Editing, Design and Bc

Editing, Design and Book Production

CHARLES FOSTER

journeyman
LONDON • BOULDER, COLORADO

First published 1993 by Journeyman Press
345 Archway Road, London N6 5AA
and 5500 Central Avenue,
Boulder, Colorado 80301, USA

British Library Cataloguing in Publication Data
A catalogue record for this book is available from the British Library

ISBN 1 85172 045 6 hb
ISBN 1 85172 046 4 pb

Designed and produced for Journeyman Press by
Chase Production Services, Chipping Norton
Typeset from author's disks by
Stanford Desktop Publishing Services, Milton Keynes
Printed in Great Britain by T.J. Press, Padstow

Contents

Acknowledgements

This short book has a long history, and is proof that publishers do not make reliable authors. I had the original idea of a comprehensive book to help hard-pressed publications officers when I was one myself, at the National Council for Civil Liberties from 1978 to 1984. Desktop publishing had not been heard of, and word processing was a source of wonderment for most. I finished a draft for InterChange Books in 1987 and the book had reached page proof stage when InterChange decided to give up publishing new titles. Journeyman then offered to publish it, but by then it needed a lot of updating – and this, too, took its time. I am grateful for Journeyman's patience.

Thanks are due to the following. Anne Beech, Linda Etchart and Diana Russell at Journeyman; Alison Clixby and Swati Patel at InterChange; Maggie Coulthard, Sarah Freeman, Paul Gordon and Lliane Phillips for helpful comments on the original draft; Janet Newman for retyping a large part of a very messy typescript; Kathryn Tattersall, Peter Hammarling, Rob Silk, Debbie Kamofsky and Rick Anderson for answering queries; Aggie MacKenzie for her contribution to the early chapters; Linotype Ltd and the Monotype Corporation Ltd for supplying specimens of typesetting.

This book probably owes most, however, to those people at the Folio Society who gave me such a good grounding in the trade and who proved time and again that quality in design, printing and production can always be achieved and is always worth the effort. They were Clive Barnes, Teresa Pemberton, John Letts, Kenneth Thompson and, particularly, Tim Wilkinson.

A book of this kind sets itself up for people to find faults or omissions. I am sure that there are some, for which I take full responsibility. I would welcome any suggestions for changes or improvements for any future editions.

This book is dedicated to the memory of my mother, who taught me not to split infinitives.

1

Introduction

Thousands and thousands of books are published each year. In the UK alone 78,835 new titles were published in 1992 and total publishers' turnover was more than £2.5 billion. At least as many pamphlets, magazines, newspapers, posters, handbills and leaflets are also produced. Despite all the predictions of the dire consequences for the printed word following the invention of electronic methods of communication, it is apparent that, for the foreseeable future at least, printing is still with us.

People like the feeling of permanence they get from a book. Solidity and respectability are somehow added to an opinion if it has been bound in a cover and found a place on a shelf. This notion is reinforced by the frequent use of filled bookshelves as a backdrop for TV appearances by politicians or academics – for even in the new media, the old medium adds an aura of responsibility and status.

So books are here to stay, more people want to communicate by producing them and it is now easier – and cheaper – than ever before to publish a book. Over the last few decades the real cost of producing printed matter has decreased and computers and desktop publishing have brought the technology of production closer to the amateur, or self-publisher.

However, there is a drawback. Because access to publishing is now relatively easy, it is also easy to make a mess of it. Hundreds of campaigning organisations, charities, trade union branches, self-publishers and writers' groups publish well-edited, designed and produced material each year. But many do not. A lot of valuable information, research, ideas and creative thought can be wasted, because they are not presented in a form easily accessible to the public. (They can also be wasted, even though excellently produced, if the material is not adequately marketed and distributed. This is outside the scope of this book, although it is covered thoroughly in a companion volume, *Marketing for Small Publishers*. See Further Reading section (pp.150–3) for details.) What this book seeks to do is to show how a knowledge of basic publishing skills can be acquired, and adapted, for use by 'small publishers'. Amongst these are all the kinds of organisations listed above, some of whom would only include publishing as part of a wider programme of activity.

Most small organisations have one thing in common. They have no shortage of people who are willing to be 'creative': to have ideas, to write material themselves, to criticise others' contributions and so on. What they often lack is someone with the practical skills necessary to get the material from an unprocessed script into a finished form. And, furthermore, someone whose job it is to remember the pictures, the cover, the publicity blurb, the list of contents and the score of other things which should at least be considered for inclusion in a finished book.

It is for this person that this book will be most useful. Someone who has been designated to produce a piece of printed matter and who has little or no experience of how to go about it. Such a person may already be working for the organisation in another capacity, such as a researcher or a librarian. Or she or he may be the person who has volunteered – or been coerced – to produce something using desktop publishing for the first time.

There are books available that teach people with little or no experience how to produce simple printed matter, such as posters, leaflets or pamphlets. There are also books which explain in great detail the technical skills of desktop publishing. And there are a number of excellent manuals written for the professionals who work in commercial publishing.

This book is different from all of these. It is a guide to the minimum skills needed to edit, design and produce a simple book or pamphlet, whether using old technology or desktop publishing. You will also find extra material on things like footnotes and references, copyright and illustrations. These may not be relevant to your particular job, but they may be useful as a reference.

The large publisher nearly always has specialist editors, designers and production staff. The small or independent publisher often cannot afford this luxury and may expect one, often overworked, person to have a number of skills. This book aims to help that person acquire those skills, so that, with practice, she or he can produce a creditable result on any reasonably straightforward job. And, I hope, it benefits from being written by someone who has served his time as the sole publications officer in a pressured and impecunious organisation, where the publishing programme was determined both by cash flow and by political necessity.

2

The Parts of a Book

Before starting work on the editing, design or production of a book, you should consider whether you have the complete typescript. The word 'typescript' is important here, since your typesetters and printers will certainly expect to work from typed matter. They may refuse – or charge you a hefty premium – if you ask them to work from anything other than typed matter (except short corrections written legibly). However, the script of a book is still often called a manuscript, or MS – just one example of the many archaisms which still crop up in publishing-speak. I have tried not to use an old term unless it is absolutely necessary. Most of the terms used in the text are defined again in the Glossary, pp.154–61.

The individual typescript can be divided into three parts: the preliminary matter, the text and the end matter. It may also contain 'figurative' matter (figures, tables and diagrams) and illustrations. If all this is present when you receive the typescript, then it is complete. If it is not, then you should consider what is missing before you process the material further.

It should be said here that for a simple pamphlet the bulk of the typescript will be just the text. There may be no call for illustrations, diagrams, index, glossary or bibliography. But there will almost certainly be a necessity for a title page and a list of contents, as well as some references or further reading or follow-up information. And if these are not present when the typescript arrives, then it is important that someone takes responsibility for compiling them.

Preliminary Matter (Prelims)

This is the collective word for all the matter appearing before the text. It is preferable that even the simplest book or pamphlet contains three pages of prelims: a title page; the back, or 'verso', of the title page containing a copyright notice, printer's imprint and bibliographical details; and a list of contents. In a larger book, the preliminary matter can get very complicated and may take up a number of pages. It could comprise any – or even all – of the following items, even though a separate page is not necessary for each:

- Half-title.
- Information about book.
- Author's biographical information.
- Series information.
- Frontispiece.
- Title page.
- Copyright notice, publishing history and bibliographical information.
- Dedication or epigraph.
- Contents list.
- Lists of illustrations, figures, maps and tables.
- List of contributors.
- Foreword.
- Preface.
- Acknowledgements.
- Lists of abbreviations.
- General figures, maps or tables relevant to the whole book.

This is the usual order. Full definitions and instructions on compiling them appear on pp.25–32. It is unlikely that the small publisher will want to include all these separate items, but it is still useful to know what they are and what functions they fulfil.

The Text

This is the bulk of the book and will probably be the part in which most of your readers are interested. This book does not go into how text should be organised or written, but you may find that you have to change or rewrite sections, particularly if the text was written by several different people. Again, how you should process the text is discussed in detail on pp.32–43.

End Matter

Just as some parts of a book appear – by use and by definition – before the main text begins, some parts usually come after. These include:

- Appendices.
- Notes and references.
- Bibliography.
- Glossary.
- Index.
- 'Advertisements' or further information.

Although some of these can be compiled and dispatched at the same time that the rest of the typescript is sent for typesetting, some cannot. For example, the index is often the last section to be completed, as it can only be compiled when the text has been 'made up' into pages with the correct 'folio' number on each page. What should go into the end matter, and how it is prepared, is also discussed below, on pp.43–53.

Figurative Matter and Illustrations

It is quite likely that any text you receive will already contain most, if not all, of the figures and tables that may be required, at least in a rough form. These require different treatment from the text and they will therefore be discussed separately (pp.53–5.)

Illustrations may or may not have been considered before you receive the text. It is usual nowadays for all illustrations, including photographs, to be printed along with the text, even if they occupy whole pages on their own. Therefore it is essential that you ascertain whether illustrations are expected before the text is processed, as this will affect how its production is handled. The number and type of illustrations will also make a large difference to the cost of production, which means you cannot get an accurate estimate from a printer without this information.

The detailed mechanics of how to handle illustrative material are dealt with in Chapter 6.

Sources
The listings of preliminary and end matter are adapted from the lists in Ruari McLean, *The Thames and Hudson Manual of Typography* (London, Thames and Hudson, 1980) and Judith Butcher, *Copy-editing: The Cambridge Handbook*, 3rd edition (Cambridge, Cambridge University Press, 1992).

3
Getting Started

The previous chapter introduced some definitions of the parts of a book and indicated how to check whether the typescript is complete. This chapter will define all the different processes a typescript will undergo before it emerges as a book.

In a commercial publishing house most of the different functions are the responsibility of separate individuals, or departments. For a small publisher, many of the functions may be carried out by the same person.

The different functions inside a publishing house are usually called the following (although the names may differ slightly from one firm to another):

- Commissioning.
- Copy-editing.
- Design.
- Production.
- Publicity.
- Marketing.
- Distribution.

Commissioning and copy-editing are sometimes lumped together under the collective title of editing.

This book is principally concerned with editing, design and production. The later chapters cover each process in detail. Here I will run through each in summary.

Commissioning

The job of the commissioning (or sponsoring) editor in a commercial publishing house is to bring together the idea for a book with the correct author and ensure that the final text is what the publisher wants.

Books come about in a variety of ways. A project may be suggested to the publisher by an author or a literary agent. Or a publisher can have an idea for a book and look for a suitable author to write it. Whichever way a book is born, it is usual for a publisher's commissioning editor to be in overall charge of a project all the way through its production. The editor looks at a synopsis and a specimen chapter, suggests changes or different approaches and liaises with the author during the writing. Fiction, too, is often now edited in this way.

Publishers also receive a lot of other material which people want to get published. It is a sad fact that most of this never sees the light of day as a book, either because it is not good enough to be published or because it is not the kind of book produced by the publisher to whom it has been sent.

When a typescript is delivered, the commissioning editor is usually the first to read it. A firm may also use outside experts to comment on its suitability, particularly if it is a specialist or academic publisher. Changes may then be suggested to the author, either of detail or more substantial matters. When the copy is satisfactory in terms of its content, the commissioning editor will pass it to the copy-editor for detailed work and correction of the typescript.

The commissioning editor will often have an important subsidiary role in dealing with the author's contract, particularly on royalties, copyright and the rights to market the title in other parts of the world, although this may be handled by a specialised department in the company.

The product of a small publisher may emerge in a slightly different way. There may be good non-commercial reasons for wanting to publish a book – for instance, to inform people of their rights, to argue a certain case or to produce fiction or poetry that is not commercially viable. There may not be a role for a traditional commissioning editor if the decision over whether or not to publish something is in the hands of, say, an executive committee. Even a small publisher, however, has some outside readers, with expertise in different fields, to comment on early drafts.

It is not the purpose of this book to go into detail about how the content of a publication should be structured. Some useful books which may give you some guidance are listed in the Further Reading section (pp.150–3).

Copy-editing

The work of the copy-editor is set out in Chapter 4. The main function is to ensure that the typesetter receives complete, clear and self-explanatory copy. This is done by detailed examination of every line of the text, and the imposition of a regularised 'house style'. This is a guide to spelling, punctuation, etc. imposed throughout a publishing house to ensure that all copy is treated consistently.

It is the responsibility of the copy-editor to provide the design and production departments with complete copy, including preliminary, end and figurative matter. It is common practice for a photocopy of the typescript to be provided to these departments while the detailed copy-editing is going on, so that initial design and estimates of production costs can be undertaken.

In a small publisher, it may be that one person is responsible for copy-editing, design and production. Although you obviously can't be doing two things at once, you may still find it useful to have a spare copy of the unedited typescript so that you can get accurate estimates. You may want to stipulate as part of the author's contract that she or he provides two copies of the typescript. (For more about estimating see p.10.)

Design

Some publishers do not have specialist designers, relying instead on the typographic skills and knowledge of their production departments. However, most large publishers, particularly those who produce heavily illustrated books, usually have a specialist department which takes responsibility for the graphic design of both books and publicity material.

An organisation may also follow a corporate 'house style' in design as well as editing. Such an approach helps readers recognise a particular publisher's products in the bookshops.

The design of a book is obviously affected, in a major way, by its overall budget. For this, and many other reasons, there is always close liaison between design and production departments.

Production

A book production department is a publisher's factory floor. It has the ultimate responsibility for the organisation's products – its books – in all matters except for their content, which is in the hands of the editorial department. This position as the lynchpin can sometimes lead to what can politely be called creative tension between the two, particularly when schedules and budgets are tight.

The production department is responsible for:

- Estimating and budgeting production costs.
- Scheduling.
- Liaison with typesetters, printers, binders and other suppliers.
- Progressing and co-ordinating work through the various suppliers, including proofreading and collating authors' proof corrections.
- Authorisation of expenditure.
- Control of the quality of the product.
- Keeping up with changes in technology and production methods.
- Design, typography and house style (if not handled by specialist designers).

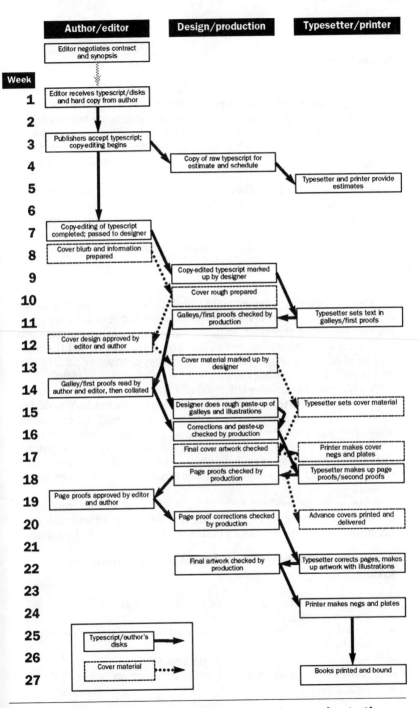

Figure 3.1. Stages in a book's production and approximate time required for each stage.

Scheduling

One of the problems of being a small publisher is that there are many times in the course of a book's production when you should be doing several things at once. This problem is even more acute when you are a very small publisher indeed – one person. It is difficult, therefore, to set out an exact order of what should be done when. The checklists on pp.145–7, and Figure 3.1 on p.9, may help you to establish the order of priorities in your own circumstances.

What should be emphasised is that you should never underestimate the time that every part of the publishing process will take you. Some approximate times for the production of an average small book (say, about 120 pages) are given in Figure 3.1. But the usual rules of life apply in publishing too – everything that *can* go wrong probably will.

Estimating

You will be able to save time in producing your book if you get estimates from typesetters and printers while the text is being copy-edited. It is useful, therefore, to have a photocopy of the complete text so that an accurate assessment of the length (or 'extent') of the book can be made. You must, of course, tell the typesetter or printer that this is only an estimating copy.

The typesetter or printer will need to know various points about the copy you supply so that an accurate estimate can be made. You do not have to make final decisions about all these matters at the estimating stage. The quotations you obtain will give you good guidance as to the price you will have to pay for having your book produced. If you are going to get comparative estimates from a number of possible suppliers then you should give them all the same basic information from which to work.

If you plan to produce your own typesetting and artwork using desktop publishing (DTP) you can still get advance estimates for printing, providing you can calculate the final extent of the book.

Information the Typesetter or Printer Will Require for Estimating

- Format: the shape and size of the book (see p.59).
- Typesize and style (see pp.69–81).
- Whether type is to be set or converted from the author's or editor's word-processing program.
- Paper and cover material (see pp.134–5).
- Number of colours used in both text and cover (see pp.138–9).
- Binding style (see pp.141–4).

- Number and type of illustrations (see pp.117–21).
- Quantity.
- Any special delivery requirements.

Choosing Printers and Other Suppliers

Commercial publishers usually buy the services they require from different suppliers so that they can use their purchasing power to make economies of scale. As a matter of course, a medium-sized commercial publisher would expect to get separate quotations for typesetting, paper, printing and binding and perhaps other services as well, such as colour origination and plate-making. The small publisher has to make a hard decision about what services to buy separately. If you only have a modest level of knowledge about the technical side of typesetting and printing (despite your detailed study of this book!), and you are not concerned about shaving a few pounds off what may not be an enormous sum of money anyway, then you may well be better advised to go to one printer who can do the whole job for you. But, for instance, you may prefer to buy the typesetting and artwork separately and liaise directly with a designer over this.

You will find that many printers are quite happy to help you with services which they don't themselves possess, such as typesetting or binding. Although they will probably charge a handling fee for organising this for you, you may well feel that it is more convenient to let the whole job go through just one pair of hands.

Alternatively, you can buy services yourself from individual freelances. Editing (both rewriting and copy-editing), design, print production and proofreading are commonly available. A useful list of freelances offering these services is available from a number of organisations listed in the Useful Organisations list, pp.148–9.

Many small publishers, particularly those with radical motives, will prefer to use printers who share similar views. Across the country there are many small and medium-sized printers, often organised as worker co-operatives or in other ways part of the radical movement. You may be able to get advice on where you can find sympathetic printers from local co-operative advisory agencies.

Casting Off

The reason for sending the complete text to the typesetter or printer is so that they can 'cast off' the typescript. This means working out exactly how long the book will be so that an accurate estimate can be made. It is worth knowing how to do a simple cast-off yourself in case it is not possible to send out a copy, or so that you can do your own estimates, based on what you know to be the cost of a similar title. (If you plan to do your own typesetting and artwork using DTP then you should be able to work out the length accurately when you import the text into the DTP program.)

In a traditionally produced typescript it is not usually enough just to calculate the number of words, since the average length of a word varies quite considerably from one text to another. It is much more accurate to count the number of characters (letters, figures, punctuation and spaces) in the complete text. This can be calculated quite easily when a text has all been typed on the same typewriter or printed by the same computer printer, unjustified, with consistent margins. The average number of characters per line is worked out, counting each letter, figure, punctuation mark and space as one character. This is multiplied by the average number of lines per page, by counting the number of lines on a few full pages, and further multiplied by the number of pages in the text. If chapters are going to start on new pages then short pages at the end of chapters are counted as full. Irregularities in the typing, such as extra space between paragraphs, the indentation of quoted matter and the treatment of subheads and footnotes, have to be assessed and compensated for.

Having established the number of characters in the text, it is then possible to work out how much space the copy will occupy. The manufacturers of typesetting equipment usually provide the users with copyfitting tables, which tell the typesetter the average number of characters that will fit on a line of a given measure. If you know which type of equipment your typesetter is using then you may be able to work how many lines of type – and therefore how many pages – your copy will make when set in a certain size to a certain measure. Specimen copyfitting tables can be seen in Figure 5.11, p.84.

If you cannot get hold of any tables you may be able to get a good estimate of the length by counting the number of characters in a sample piece of setting of the typeface in the size and measure you plan to use, produced by the typesetter. It is not a good idea to use a sample from a different typesetter to work out the number of characters per line, since there is considerable variation between equipment, and indeed between users. Figure 3.2, p.13, shows a specimen page of cast-off typescript.

To work out how many pages there will be in your book you must also allow for the space occupied by the preliminary pages, the end matter and the illustrations. A normal format book will probably be printed in sections of eight, 16 or 32 pages, so you should round this final figure up to a multiple of eight. You should now be able to estimate the final length of the book to within a 10 per cent margin of error. Before you congratulate yourself too heartily on how you've managed to do this, bear in mind that a trained estimator would expect to cast off a manuscript to within 1 per cent!

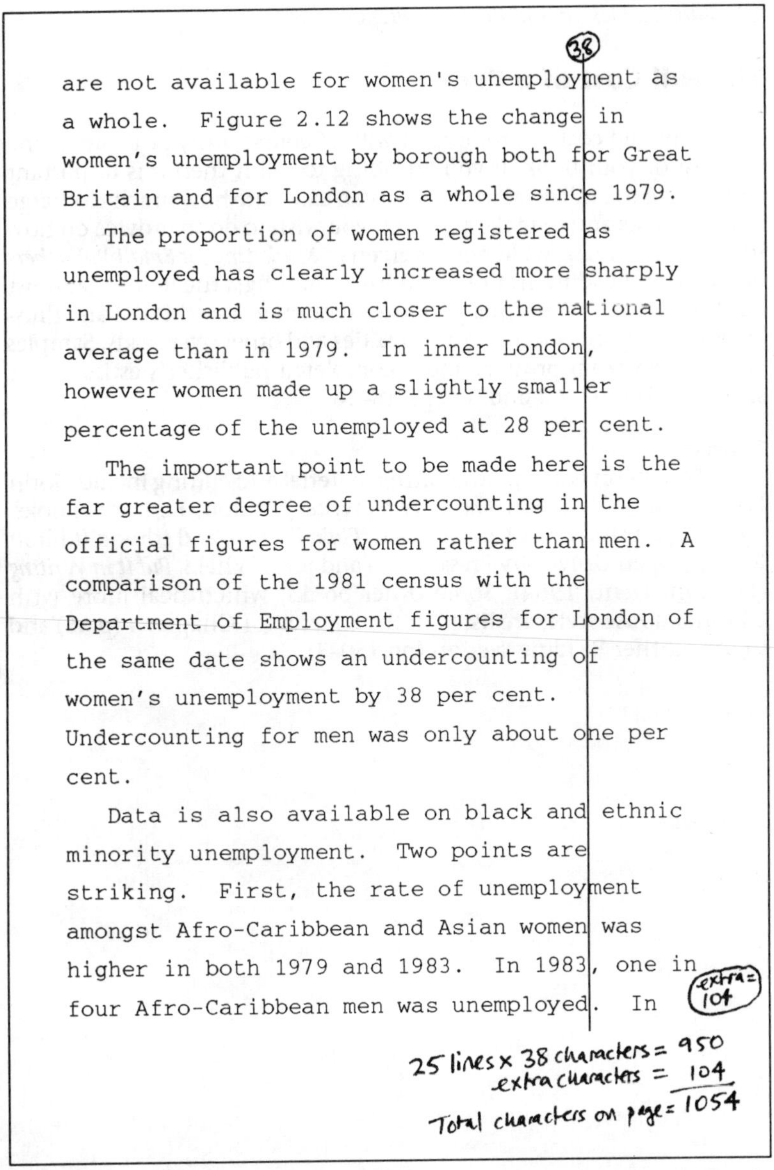

are not available for women's unemployment as a whole. Figure 2.12 shows the change in women's unemployment by borough both for Great Britain and for London as a whole since 1979.

The proportion of women registered as unemployed has clearly increased more sharply in London and is much closer to the national average than in 1979. In inner London, however women made up a slightly smaller percentage of the unemployed at 28 per cent.

The important point to be made here is the far greater degree of undercounting in the official figures for women rather than men. A comparison of the 1981 census with the Department of Employment figures for London of the same date shows an undercounting of women's unemployment by 38 per cent. Undercounting for men was only about one per cent.

Data is also available on black and ethnic minority unemployment. Two points are striking. First, the rate of unemployment amongst Afro-Caribbean and Asian women was higher in both 1979 and 1983. In 1983, one in four Afro-Caribbean men was unemployed. In

extra = 104

25 lines × 38 characters = 950
extra characters = 104
Total characters on page = 1054

Figure 3.2. Casting off a typescript. A vertical line is drawn on a sample page, aligned with the shortest full line. All the extra characters, spaces and figures are then counted to calculate the exact number of characters on the page. This exercise is repeated on several pages to get an average figure, and then the total number of characters in the typescript can be calculated.

The Full Cost of a Book

The estimated cost of production will, of course, only be a part of the full cost of your book. If you are going to sell it then it is important to estimate the full cost, so that you can calculate how much to charge to cover costs and to make a profit if you wish to do so. Advice on how to work out a reasonable price is given in *Marketing for Small Publishers* (see Further Reading section, pp.150–3). Amongst the items that must be allowed for in your final publisher's estimate are editorial and illustration fees, promotional costs, royalties and other overheads. Samples of estimates from printers and a completed publisher's estimate are shown in Figures 3.3 and 3.4, pp.15–16.

Sources
Useful books on writing, structuring material and editing include John Fairfax and John Moat, *The Way to Write* (London, Elm Tree Books, 1981), Open University Course Team, *Plain English*, 2nd edition (Milton Keynes, Open University Press, 1982) and John Whale, *Put It in Writing* (London, Dent, 1984). Some other books, which deal more with editorial house style, are listed in the Sources for Chapter 4 (p.55) and in the Further Reading section (pp.150–3).

Inky and Smudge Ltd

Printers and Binders
123 Updown Street
London SE32 1PG
Tel 081-234 5678

Ms J Jones
Small Publishing Co-op
456 Worthy Road
London N29 9KL

15 September 1992

Dear Ms Jones

Council Tenants Rights Guide

Thank you for your enquiry. We are pleased to submit our quotation as follows.

Typesetting 20,000 words in 11/12pt Plantin Medium. Supplying galley proofs. Making up into page from your rough paste-up, including 12 line illustrations reduced from original artwork.

Printing 24pp A4 in black only on 90gsm white cartridge. Cover printed in black plus two colours on one side only on 240gsm Trulux board, from complete artwork supplied.

Folded, saddle stitched two wires, trimmed.

2,000 copies   £2250
1,000 copies run on   £210

Inclusive of bulk delivery to one London address.

We hope that this meets with your approval.

Yours sincerely

Susan Charming
Sales Representative

See over for our standard conditions of contract.

Figure 3.3. Estimate from a printer.

Small Publishing Co-op
456 Worthy Road
London N29 9KL

Estimated costs

Title _Council Tenants Rights_ Author _Jones_

	Print run	1000	2000	3000
EDITORIAL				
Author's fees	Contribn. to research fees	250	250	250
Copy-editing	In house	—	—	—
Permissions	None	—	—	—
Other				
DESIGN/TYPESETTING				
Designer	In house	—	—	—
Artist	Sally Smith: 6 cartoons	240	240	240
Permissions	None	—	—	—
Artwork costs	Ace DTP: 24pp A4	1200	1200	1200
Other				
PRINTING/BINDING				
Printing text	Inky + Smudge	600	720	840
Printing cover	"	200	240	280
Cover design/artwork	Raj Kumar	150	150	150
Binding - paper	Inky + Smudge	150	180	210
cloth		—	—	—
Other				
TOTAL		2790	2980	3170
Unit cost		£2.79	£1.49	£1.06

AUTHOR'S ROYALTY _7½%_

Figure 3.4. Publisher's estimate for editorial and production costs.
Editorial, design and typesetting costs are usually constant
whatever the print run. However because the unit print cost goes
down as the run goes up, the overall unit cost is reduced.

4

Editing

Preparation of the Typescript

Four different kinds of work will be done on a typescript before the typesetter sets a single word in type. These are editing, copy-editing, typographical design and typesetter's mark-up. With a small publisher, one person may well be solely responsible for most – or all – of these functions. If this is the case it is possible, to a certain extent, to cut some corners and you should not need to read the typescript in detail more than once. But you will also find it a lot easier to handle each of these functions in order and not attempt, for instance, to design the text at the same time as you copy-edit it.

Editing with Computer-generated Text

Many more authors now use computers and word processing programs for writing, and supply their copy on floppy disk as well as on paper (sometimes called 'hard copy'). The copy-editor may therefore either work directly on disk on the author's text, or mark the typescript and expect the author or typesetter to make the corrections.

If you are planning to use the disk the author supplies – either yourself, if you are using your own desktop publishing facilities, or to send to the typesetters – then you need to discuss this with the author at an early stage. She or he will need clear instructions on how you want the text prepared. This is dealt with further in Chapter 7.

With desktop publishing you can, in theory, do all your editing on screen, without ever producing copy on paper. You might, however, find this very hard on your eyes. And even the highest resolution computer monitors do not reproduce type completely accurately – so you might well miss details which you will see on paper.

For the same reason, even if you plan to edit the text on screen using a word processing program, you may still find it easier to work with hard copy, at least part of the time. You work through the text, in the same way as you would with a typescript, and then transfer the corrections onto the computer. You can, of course, also use any special functions your computer program offers, such as 'search and replace', to cut down on some mundane tasks.

What Copy-editing Entails

As mentioned before, it is not the purpose of this book to go into detail about how a publication should be structured editorially. In a commercial publishing house this would be the work of a commissioning or sponsoring editor, who would discuss with the author the content, scope and organisation of the text. I am assuming that the typescript has reached you in a form with which both you and any others involved in the commissioning process are happy. The major task with which you will be involved is copy-editing, a process which should have unobtrusive results. The aim of the copy-editor should be similar to the aim of the designer: to remove any obstacles between the reader and what the author is trying to say and then to express this message in a clear form. Your work is picked up unconsciously by your readers – they do not see what you have done if it is done thoroughly, but they notice if it is not.

The main function of the copy-editor is to ensure that the typesetter receives complete, clear and self-explanatory copy. The pages of the typescript must be numbered in sequence, the various kinds of heading and passages that need to be distinguished typographically have to be identified, and corrections or additions must be made in the correct place. Illustrations and figurative material have to be assessed and if they are to be cross-referenced with the text these references have to be prepared.

It would be quite impossible to list here all the things you should do. In Judith Butcher's book *Copy-editing*, the definitive manual on the subject (see Further Reading section, pp.150–3), the checklist of 'the most obvious things' contains nearly 300 items! A much shorter checklist appears on pp.145–7 of this book and you might find it useful to adapt this for your own use.

The most important principle is that of consistency. Most large publishers have their own guides to 'house style' so that their editorial staff can ensure that each book follows a constant pattern in spelling, use of capitals, italics, punctuation, etc. You may find it useful to produce your own house style guide (see pp.19–21). Most of the rules laid down in anyone's house style are simply to maintain this first rule of copy-editing: be consistent.

The second rule is: treat your readers as though they are unfamiliar with the subject. While you can probably assume that a UK reader will know what the initials BBC or TUC stand for, there are other abbreviations that must be spelled out, at least at their first mention. Your authors may well have assumed a level of knowledge which some of your readers will not possess.

The third rule is: know your grammar and spelling. If you cannot tell the difference between 'it's' and 'its', and 'affect' and 'effect', then you will certainly have to find out before taking up copy-editing seriously. You will quickly find out that many authors do not know! Some useful books on usage and grammar can be found in the Further Reading section (pp.150–3).

House Style Guide

If you are publishing anything – books, pamphlets or journals – on a regular basis, then you will certainly save everyone time and money if you produce a simple guide for authors to show how you want them to type and lay out their scripts. If you do this, then, with luck, you will get beautifully typed scripts back. Thus you will save yourself hours of laborious work, whether on paper or on screen, on such tasks as replacing double quotation marks (" ") with single ('). Experience shows that this style guide should be kept quite simple. Authors, as a breed, are highly likely to find a very detailed guide listing every eventuality far too complicated to understand. They then ignore the whole thing.

A sample list of points and a sample guide to the layout of typescripts appear in Figures 4.1 and 4.2, pp.20 and 21.

There may be reasons why you should produce a longer house style. These include being engaged in regular publishing, or if other people (say, volunteers or freelances) work with you, or if you occasionally produce more complicated books with, for instance, lots of references. If you are intending to produce your own artwork using desktop publishing then such a guide will also be necessary. You will find advice on the items that you might want to include in a more wide-ranging guide in the section on preparing the text (pp.32–43).

When the Typescript Arrives

If you have been able to intervene before the typescript arrives, and you have read the preceding pages of this book, then you should have a relatively easy job in copy-editing the text. But in an unfair world, one of the lesser injustices is the inability of authors and commissioning editors to make life easy for copy-editors and production staff, and you may find that your typescript presents you with a lot of problems. It may have been typed by someone who has never been taught to type at all, with a host of horrific idiosyncrasies. Even some professional journalists or writers seem to take a perverse pride in turning in almost uncorrected scripts which look as though they have been produced by a child on a toy machine. Word processing may have reduced the number of mistakes that some people make in their typing but it has by no means eliminated them.

Small Publishing Co-op
456 Worthy Road
London N29 9KL

Guidelines on House Style

In order to help our copy-editors we ask all authors to follow these guidelines when typing or word processing copy for publication. In this way we can minimise delays and costs, and ensure a consistent house style.

1. Do not use full points in abbreviations - such as BBC, TUC, Mr, St - except in the very common Latin abbreviations such as e.g., i.e. and etc.

2. Do not use apostrophes in plurals - MPs, the 1980s.

3. Do not use unnecessary initial capitals. Words like government, court, judge, do not need them. But a specific job title, as in 'Kenneth Clarke, the Home Secretary,...', does.

4. Use the style Thursday 10 December 1992 for dates (note - no commas).

5. Check that the hyphenation of compound words is consistent.

6. Do not underline, embolden or italicise any text unless you are sure it is going to be set in italic type in the printed book. This normally applies only to unusual words in languages other than English, book titles etc.

7. Spell out all numbers from one to ten. Use figures for numbers from 11 upwards.

8. Use per cent, not the symbol %, in text (but use % in tables).

9. Use single quotation marks (') not double (") for all quoted matter, except for quotes within quotes where you should use double.

10. If using footnotes and references, consult the copy-editor about the system you are using - and be consistent.

Figure 4.1. House style points for authors.

Small Publishing Co-op
456 Worthy Road
London N29 9KL

Producing the typescript/word processed
hard copy.

1. Set generous margins: at least 3 cm on
left and 4 cm on right, at head and at foot.

2. Type on one side of the paper only.

3. Type all copy double spaced, with one
extra double space between paragraphs.

4. Do not indent paragraphs.

5. Do not use justification (even left and
right margins).

6. Start each new chapter or major section
on a new page.

7. Number the pages of the whole typescript
in one continuous sequence.

8. Even if you are supplying a copy of the
text on disk for us to process, we still
need a complete hard copy of all the text.
Please ensure that the print out is exactly
the same as the text on disk.

Figure 4.2. Typing guidelines for authors.

If the script is in such a poor state that it has to be retyped then ensure that major inconsistencies of style are dealt with while this occurs – say, changing double to single quotes or changing the numbering sequence of footnotes. But you should not do major work on a typescript before it is retyped since you will only have to read the whole thing again when it comes back.

Writing to the Author

After your first look through the typescript and before you begin your detailed corrections you will probably find it helpful to write to the author or have a meeting with him or her to discuss general and specific points. You should mention things like capitalisation and punctuation if you think you are going to change them, in case there is some specific reason for the author's own style. You may want to raise some or all of the following items:

- Chapter titles and numbering.
- Subheadings, particularly if the author has devised an over-complicated system.
- Page headlines or running heads (if you are going to use them).
- Notes: how they are to be numbered, whether they are to be footnotes or endnotes and whether they will be placed at the end of the chapter or of the whole book.
- Quoted matter: how it will be distinguished.
- Figurative matter: numbering of tables and figures, as they will not necessarily fall where they do in the typescript.
- Illustrations: quantity and type.
- References: the system used.
- Cross-references: if there are too many or if archaic forms are used, such as *post* or *supra*.
- Numbers.
- Dates.
- Abbreviations.

If an author is uneasy about what you are going to do to the typescript and you decide to send her or him a copy of it when you have finished, then tell the author to make any marks in ink of a different colour from yours so that you can check them when it comes back.

You should try to get an assurance that major parts of the text are not going to be rewritten when the author receives proofs of the typeset text, although this may be difficult.

You may wish to raise with the author that the text could better promote equal opportunities for women, black and other ethnic community people, lesbians and gay men, older and younger people and people with disabilities. This is discussed later, on pp.41–3.

How to Begin Copy-editing

The real work on a text comes when you have had your first discussion with the author. You are now ready to begin the painstaking work of reading through the typescript, noting and marking every inconsistency and turning it into copy that the printer can follow easily.

Although the text may be looked through again, by a designer and a typesetter, this is probably the only time that it will be read in so much detail. Indeed, if the book is the product of several hands then this may be the first time that it has been read so carefully, which means that you might turn up more than you expect!

For this reason, even if you are the person who is also going to design and mark-up or typeset the text, you should concentrate on copy-editing at this stage. You will find it easier if you can set aside enough time to work through the text continuously. If you leave it for several weeks between bouts of activity then you may miss minor inconsistencies.

How to Mark the Typescript

If the typesetter is to work quickly and economically then she or he must be able to read straight down each sheet of the typescript, which will probably be clipped in a special holder by the side of the keyboard. Flaps of paper will hide what is written underneath, additions written sideways in the margin will mean that the paper has to be turned, instructions to take paragraphs forward or back from different sheets will mean further delay. The occasional addition is acceptable if it is marked clearly on which page of the typescript it falls, it is typed on a single sheet of full-size paper and directly follows the page it adds to. You should take time retyping if necessary and getting the pages in the correct order. Half sheets of paper should be repasted on to full sheets and new material to be fastened over old material should be pasted down rather than clipped or stapled. It is much better, say, to have six full-size sheets of paper, each with one or two paragraphs all in the correct order, than three with paragraphs to be moved around, plus a couple of odd half sheets with other sections.

Do not, ever, write copy on the back of a sheet. It is very inconvenient for the typesetter and also makes photocopying the typescript more difficult.

Check that all handwritten material – especially proper names, unfamiliar words and potentially ambiguous characters – is legible. Whatever you mark on the typescript must be marked throughout. You cannot just mark the first few instances, or occasional instances as a reminder, as the book will probably be set by more than one operator. Use the same marks as for proof correction (see pp.108–11).

The following should be marked in the left-hand margin:

- 'Fresh page' or 'right-hand page' when you want this to occur in the final book.
- Codes for subheadings, usually with a pencil letter in a square (see p.41).
- Vertical lines where quoted matter is to be set either indented or in a different type size; see that the beginning and end of such passages are made clear.
- Instructions as to where illustrations and figurative matter are to fall.
- ⌐⌐ to indicate a new paragraph where this is not clear on the typescript.

All other marks should be *between the lines* of the typescript if there is room to write them clearly, rather than in the margin, as you would do for proofs. This is because the typesetter reads the typescript word by word and going over to the margin to read corrections slows her or him down. (When correcting proofs, on the other hand, the typesetter just looks down the margins for which lines need correction and does not look at the text until a marginal mark is found.)

So you do not need to use the marginal marks for such instructions as deletion, transposition, italic, bold, roman, capitals, lower case, close up, run on, or space. Em or en rules (long or short dashes) and hyphens should be marked with 'em', 'en' and 'hyphen' written above the typescript dash (for explanation of these see pp.38–9). (To reduce confusion, word-processing programs should be used with the hyphenation function turned off if possible.)

You have a further tool at your disposal in marking typewriter-produced typescripts which you must never use either for deleting or changing type on the paper copy of computer-generated copy or for correcting proofs: white-out fluid. Do not be frightened of using this, since it will make the typescript a lot less ambiguous for the typesetter. It is invaluable for such functions as cancelling underlining and turning double quotes into single, and on paper copy of computer-generated copy for deleting incorrect proofing or editing marks. (Avoid breathing in the fumes which in most brands are a health hazard.)

The pages of the typescript should all be numbered in one sequence, not by chapter, so that it can be easily reassembled if it is broken up by the typesetters to be given to more than one operator – or if you drop it on the floor. If some pages are added later they should be numbered as, say, pages 123a and 123b, and inserted in the typescript after page 123. A note should be written on page 123 saying 'pages 123a and 123b follow'. Similarly if pages are removed then a note should be made on the page immediately preceding the sequence, 'pages 88–93 missing – page 94 follows.'

A specimen of a fully copy-edited page is shown in Figure 4.3, p.26.

Preparing the Prelims

As mentioned previously (p.3), even the simplest book or pamphlet is improved with the provision of some rudimentary preliminary pages to give readers details of the title and contents before the text begins. More complicated books may contain other preliminary matter.

The preliminary pages can be prepared after the text itself has been copy-edited. The typesetters can then begin work on setting the text while this is going on. If you are going to do this, then it is helpful to the typesetters if you give them a list of the prelims that you are preparing and an estimate of the number of pages each of them will take up. If you are sure that these estimates are accurate, then the text can be made up into pages while the prelims are being prepared. In commercial publishing this is common practice, and the prelims are often numbered with roman numerals (i, ii, iii, etc.) while the text itself begins the arabic numeral sequence (1, 2, 3, etc.). Thus there is no need for renumbering either if there is more preliminary matter than first thought, or if extra prelims are thought to be likely in the case of a reprint. You may however think that it is an unnecessary luxury to number your prelims with a roman numeral sequence – and it would certainly look a little pretentious in a 16-page pamphlet!

You should prepare complete copy for all the prelims you are going to include. This includes such things as the name and address of the publisher, and the names and localities of the typesetter and printer.

Half-title

The main title page of a book is usually preceded by the half-title page. This is so called because it often contains only the title of the book and any series it comes from, leaving the author's and publisher's names and so on to appear on the full title page. It has a number of functions. First of all it acts as an identifier when books are stacked in the bindery, after they have been folded and collated but before they are bound. The title page is also protected at this delicate stage by the half-title, which is important if you are producing expensive books with ornate or decorated title pages. Secondly, the binding process for both cased and paperback books involves glueing the first and last pages either to an endpaper or to the cover material itself. This means that the first page of a book may be difficult to open fully and may be marred with glue seeping down the edge. It is sensible therefore not to have the title page as the first page of the book. In a pamphlet bound with wire

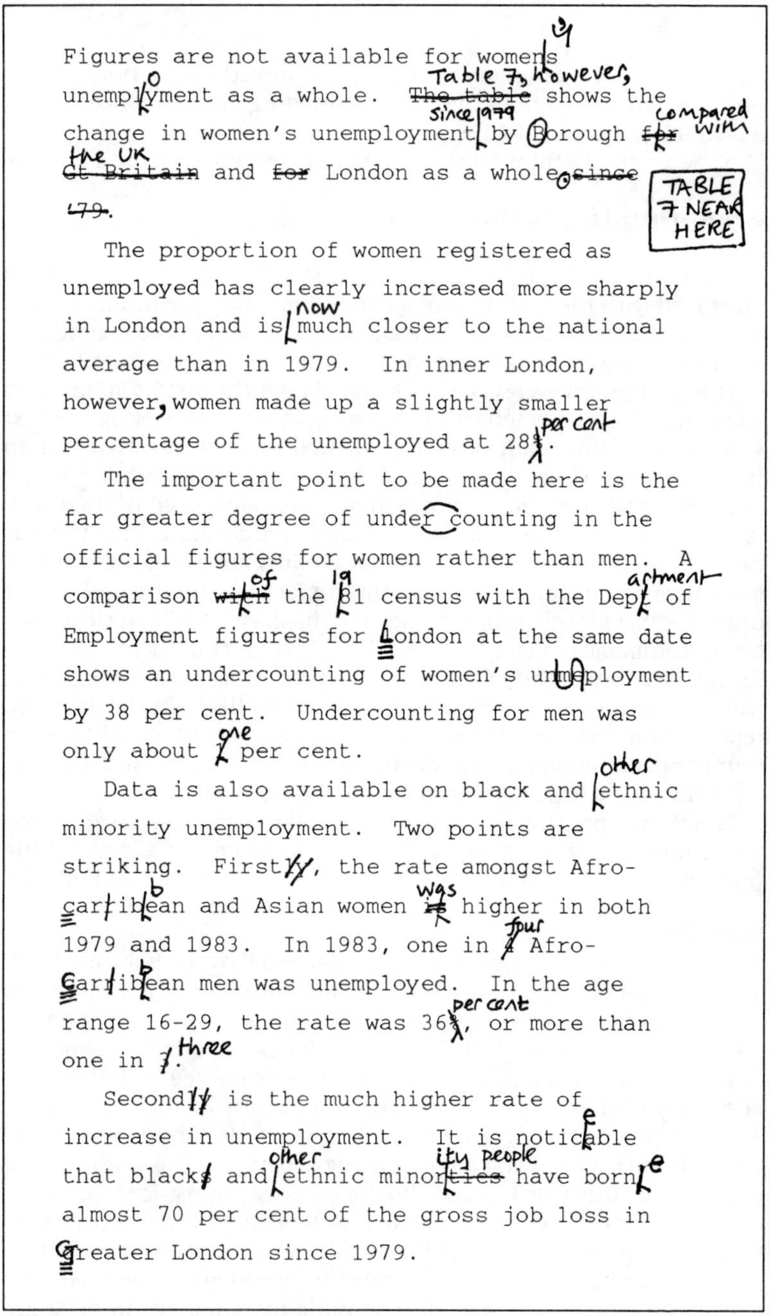

Figures are not available for women's unemployment as a whole. Table 7, however, shows the change in women's unemployment since 1979 by Borough compared with the UK and London as a whole.

The proportion of women registered as unemployed has clearly increased more sharply in London and is now much closer to the national average than in 1979. In inner London, however, women made up a slightly smaller percentage of the unemployed at 28 per cent.

The important point to be made here is the far greater degree of under counting in the official figures for women rather than men. A comparison of the 1981 census with the Department of Employment figures for London at the same date shows an undercounting of women's unemployment by 38 per cent. Undercounting for men was only about one per cent.

Data is also available on black and other ethnic minority unemployment. Two points are striking. First, the rate amongst Afro-Caribbean and Asian women was higher in both 1979 and 1983. In 1983, one in four Afro-Caribbean men was unemployed. In the age range 16-29, the rate was 36 per cent, or more than one in three.

Second is the much higher rate of increase in unemployment. It is noticeable that black and other ethnic minority people have borne almost 70 per cent of the gross job loss in Greater London since 1979.

Figure 4.3. A page of fully copy-edited text.

staples in the spine ('wire saddle stitched'), the first page will lie flat and it may therefore be unnecessary to have a special half-title page.

The half-title also has some other useful functions. It provides a convenient place for such things as blurbs, series information and authors' biographies. If your book is a second edition, or a paperback version of a previously published hardback, then this page can also be used for extracts from reviews.

Half-title Verso

In printing and publishing left-hand pages are called 'versos' and right-hand pages 'rectos'. If you have a half-title then the reverse of this page, the first left-hand page in the book, is called the 'half-title verso'. An illustration on this page is called a 'frontispiece'. If there is no illustration here then this page may be used for a list of other books by the author or other books in the same series.

Title Page

For centuries, designers have used the title page to display their typographic skill. We will come to how it should be designed later (see pp.86–7). Preparing the copy itself for the designer or printer should be a simpler task.

The title, style for series and volume number, form of author's name and description should be the same as on the half-title and on any brief that is going to a cover designer. It is not at all uncommon for mistakes to be made, leading to different versions of the title appearing on the cover and on the title page – so check this carefully.

It is unnecessary to have any punctuation between the title and any subtitle (although they are usually separated by a dash or a colon when they are listed in bibliographies).

The names of any translators, artists or foreword-writers should also appear on the title page. The number of the edition should be given, if it is not the first (see p.29). The publisher's name, device or logo should also appear. The year of publication and town or city are sometimes included, but this is not essential providing full details are given on the next page.

Title-page Verso

This is the traditional page for all the important data about a book which will mean that it is properly catalogued and listed in libraries and bibliographies. Too often, small publishers omit information which should be supplied here, which means that it is difficult for others to trace the publication at a later stage. The following should be included:

The Publisher's Name and Full Address This should also include the address of any co-publisher for overseas markets.

Copyright Notice The law on copyright is very complicated, and you should always seek permission to reproduce someone else's copyright material. To establish your copyright for the book you are publishing all you have to do is to print the copyright symbol © and state the copyright proprietor (usually either the author or the publisher) and the year of publication.

It is also becoming standard practice, following the Copyright, Designs and Patents Act 1988, to include the line: 'The right of [author's name] to be identified as the author of this work has been asserted by [her, him, them] in accordance with the Copyright, Designs and Patents Act 1988.' In order for this right to be claimed, the author must first sign a declaration to that effect. The 'moral right' line should appear immediately after the copyright © line.

There are two exceptions where you cannot use the © copyright symbol. The first is when you are reprinting a work which was originally published before the country of publication became a signatory to the Universal Copyright Convention (the UCC). The UK signed this on 27 September 1957. But if your work contains a new introduction or other material not in the original edition then you can establish copyright on that, simply by printing the publisher or author's name:

Introduction © Joan Baptiste, 1988

If the edition is significantly different from a work published before 1957 – an edited or updated version, say – then it is permissible to establish copyright on the whole text.

The second case where a © symbol cannot be used only arises with books written in the USA before the US Copyright Act of 1976 and imported for sale into the USA. If this applies to your title, you should seek specialist advice.

There are a few other points that you should watch out for on the copyright line.

If you are publishing the first British edition of a book first published in the USA then the copyright date should be the date of first publication, or registration at the Library of Congress, in the USA.

If the book is a translation, then there may be two notices: one for the original, if it is still in copyright, and one for the translation.

An edition of a text has a copyright notice for the text, if it is still in copyright, and another for the editorial material.

An anthology requires acknowledgements for the original items and a copyright notice which establishes copyright on the other matter and the selection of items. It might read:

Introduction, selection and notes © Arthur Smith, 1988

When you are printing or publishing a new edition of a work you have already published then the notice will have to be modified.

Anti-copyright Some publishers make a positive statement that their work is copyright-free, stating that it can be reproduced by anyone who does not want to use it for profit or exploitation, etc. It may be better not to take such a radical step since it is always possible to give someone permission to use your work for free if you are sympathetic to their motives. It would, on the other hand, be difficult to stop someone using your work once you had made such a bold and sweeping statement. In addition, it is an arguable point that since you establish copyright on something merely by publishing it, even if you do not bother to put a copyright notice on it, you cannot dispose of it as simply as that!

Publishing History and Date If this is the first edition, then all you need put is: first published, year. If you are not the original publisher then you should say who that was, and the year of original publication. You may want to list all the impressions and editions that have been published. A book which is reprinted without amendment or with only a few corrections or updates is called a new impression. Substantial changes are acknowledged by calling the book a new edition.

A practice which is becoming more common is to typeset a line on the verso incorporating both years and impression numbers, in the style:

$$95 \quad 94 \quad 93 \quad 92 \quad 1 \quad 2 \quad 3 \quad 4$$

The central numbers indicate the impression number and the year – in this case, First impression 1992. If a second impression takes place in 1994 deletions are made to the plate so that it reads:

$$95 \quad 94 \qquad\qquad 2 \quad 3 \quad 4$$

This method saves the cost of resetting type and making a new plate just to incorporate an impression number.

If the title is a translation then the original title, date and publisher's name and address should be given.

International Standard Book Number (ISBN) An International Standard Book Number is a unique number used to identify every edition of every title. The system is widely used by booksellers and librarians for ordering, and allocation of a number ensures listing in the standard reference book *British Books in Print.* The ISBN is a 10-digit number which you allocate to your book yourself from a list you can get from the Standard Book Numbering Agency. Every publisher is given a unique prefix – and if you are a new publisher you should apply to the Agency for a prefix. If you are a small publisher (under about six titles per year) the Agency will also allocate individual book numbers on the telephone for you while you wait. Full details of how the numbers are calculated are available from the Agency, or in *Copy-editing* by Judith Butcher (pp.175–6). The Standard Book Numbering Agency's address is given in the Useful Organisations list, p.148.

There is a different ISBN for each edition and binding of each book so if you are going to divide up your book after printing into, say, both cased and paperback bound editions then you need to print both ISBNs on the title-page verso, making clear which number belongs to which binding. The number should also appear at the base of the back cover or jacket and here should be only the number that relates to the particular binding. The ISBN is also used to prepare the unique barcode, which should appear on the cover or jacket of any book or pamphlet to be sold commercially. (See p.97 for more about barcodes.)

Cataloguing in Publication Data (CIP) This is a set of numbers and words describing your book for bibliographers and librarians, enabling them to catalogue it more quickly. The British Library has awarded the book listing company J. Whitaker the contract for supplying the British Library with CIP records of all forthcoming titles. Publishers supply Whitaker with information on every forthcoming title on blue Whitaker Book Information forms – used for its listings – and it supplies the appropriate information to the British Library. The publisher no longer prints the CIP block on the title-page verso but simply inserts the copy:

British Library Cataloguing in Publication Data
A catalogue record for this book is available from the British Library.

Further information can be obtained from J. Whitaker, listed in Useful Organisations, p.149.

Printers' Details The name of the printers should be given. By law, you should give the address also but it is usual just to say 'Printed in Great Britain (or wherever) by XXXX Printers Ltd, Town'. You may want to include other credits for typesetters, binders and other suppliers.

Dedication or Epigraph
Traditionalists say that these should have a page to themselves and the increasing clutter now usually present on the title-page verso makes it difficult to place something so personal there. Whether you can afford two pages straight after the title-page verso (since the verso of the dedication cannot really be used to start the list of contents) will be something that only you, your designer and your budget can decide. You may be lucky and find that the last page of the prelims ends on a recto, so that the verso facing the first page of the text can

be used for the dedication or epigraph. If this is so, then this is probably a good compromise.

Contents

All non-fiction books should contain a list of contents. Many authors of short books or pamphlets do not bother to compile one. If a list of contents has not been included, then you should compile one, as it will be helpful to the reader.

The heading should be 'Contents', not 'Contents List', 'Table of Contents', etc.

The contents list should contain all the preliminary matter except the half title, half-title verso, title page, title-page verso, dedication and epigraph. Lists of illustrations and figurative material are called 'List of illustrations', 'List of figures', etc. in the contents list although on the page on which they appear, their heading may be just 'Illustrations', 'Figures', etc. If the foreword has been written by someone other than the author then that name should appear in the list. The contents list should also contain all the end matter.

The contents list should not be over-detailed. If your book contains more than one grade of subheading then try to confine the contents list to just the major series.

See that all parts, chapters and the subheadings of the relevant grade appear in the list, and that they tally with the text and with each other. The word 'part' is usually retained in contents lists, but the word 'chapter' is superfluous and need not appear. If there is more than one appendix then you can delete the word 'appendix' before each one providing you add 'appendices' above the first. In a multi-authored book the individual authors should be given against the chapters. You should write (00) after each item in the list so that the designer remembers to allow for the page numbers when marking up the copy. (You cannot, of course, set the actual numbers until the page proofs have arrived and been checked.)

Other Lists

The heading to each of these lists should be 'Illustrations', 'Figures', 'Contributors', etc. If the illustrations have been printed along with the text then these should be numbered in with the text and the numbers given in the list. The style 'facing page 123' is only used when the illustrations have been printed separately and bound in, which is rare nowadays.

Check that all the copy in the lists tallies with the captions or headings to which it refers. If these are very long when they appear in the book, then shortened versions can be used. You may want to put the acknowledgements of the sources of illustrations either in the list or in the caption next to the relevant picture.

In general, there is no particular need for a large number of lists in the prelims, other than the contents list, unless you and the author think that it would be helpful to the reader.

Foreword, Preface and Introduction

There is sometimes confusion about the difference between these. Cambridge University Press defines the terms broadly as follows.[1] The *preface* is the author's account of the scope and purpose of the book, how it came to be written and any acknowledgements of assistance. The *foreword* may be written by the author or someone else, and touches on the subject matter in a general way, relating it to other work in the same field, as a stimulus to what is to come. An *introduction* deals wholly with the subject matter of the book. If it serves merely as a general preamble to the text then it should be in the prelims. If it is vital to the comprehension of the text then it should be lifted out of the prelims and appear before the first chapter or, indeed, as the first chapter.

If acknowledgements are not part of the preface then they should be listed separately. Acknowledgements of sources of material covered by copyright are best listed separately, unless each one is listed immediately after it appears in the text.

List of Abbreviations, Notes on Sources, etc.

This should be placed as near as possible to the beginning of the text, preferably on a left-hand page, since this is easier for the reader to turn back to. Again, this should be checked with the text itself, to make sure that abbreviations, etc. are consistent. If you think an explanatory note to the author's system is required and the author has not supplied one then it is probably easier for you to do it yourself and send it to her or him, since you are the person who has to make sure that it is consistent with the text.

Preparing the Text

Before you begin work on the text it may have been possible for you to have met or written to the author. If you have done this and resolved the points discussed earlier (see p.22), then the imposition of a consistent style in the text may not be too difficult.

But even if this is so, and you have a developed house style of your own, it will still not cover every spelling, hyphen or capital. So you should keep a running style sheet as you go through the text with a note of particular spellings, capitalisations, type of cross-referencing and so on, with a note of the page on which particular items fall, so that you can check back at a later stage. An example of the kind of running style sheet you might find useful is in Figure 4.4, opposite.

Title: Working London	Author: Brown

A–D	**E–H**
the <u>City</u> (of London only) bypass co-operate (but uncooperative) BBC	the government <u>Conservative</u> government flexitime

I–L	**M–P**
inquiry in so far -ise endings Lloyd's of London Lloyds Bank	overtime part-time, full-time post-war, pre-war Numbers 1–10 1984-5 (1 _N_ 1 dash)

Q–T	**U–Z**
<u>Third World</u> <u>Second World War</u> three-quarters quotes: single ' ' <u>Stock Exchange</u> trade union (noun) trade-union (adj.)	white-collar (adj.) UK USA (US as adj. only)

Figure 4.4. Running style sheet, divided alphabetically.

It would, as mentioned earlier, be impossible to list all the things that you might have to do with the text as you go through it. A checklist appears on pp.145–7, which you may find useful when you begin to work through a text. The next section of this book deals with a few of the common problems which you may well come across. It is derived largely from the much fuller advice given in three very helpful books which you may want to consult further. These are *Copy-editing* by Judith Butcher, *Hart's Rules* and the *Chicago Manual of Style*. Full details are given in the Further Reading section, pp.150–3.

Abbreviations

If you are in any doubt whether an abbreviation will be understood then it should be spelled out, at least at the first mention. Subsequent mentions can use an abbreviation that has been introduced in parentheses at the first mention. So you would say 'the Transport and General Workers Union (TGWU)' at the first mention and then use 'TGWU' thereafter. The level at which you can assume general knowledge of any abbreviation is up to you to decide, but I would stick to very familiar ones such as BBC, MP or TUC.

Most publishers omit full points (full stops) in sets of initials and also in contractions, which are abbreviations including the first and last letter of the singular. Thus we get NATO, CND, Mr, St. The only common exception is No. for number, which is given a full point to avoid ambiguity. Per cent should not be given a full point and should be spelled out in the text, rather than using the % symbol.

Apostrophes are not necessary in plurals such as MPs.

Italics should be used when words normally set in italic type are shortened, such as book or journal names in references. (See italic and roman type, pp.36–7.) Very common foreign abbreviations, such as e.g. and i.e., are not italicised.

A second full point is not necessary when an abbreviation ends a sentence.

Do not use an ampersand (&), except in the names of firms where it is the correct style. It can, however, be used in an index or table to save space.

Capitalisation

In general avoid unnecessary capitalisation. The author may have used a perfectly acceptable system which she or he is happy with. If it is consistent then you should follow it.

It is usual to capitalise:

- Titles and ranks: King George, the Bishop of Durham, but not 'several bishops have expressed interest'.
- Institutions, movements and political parties: House of Commons, Marxism, the Labour Party, but not 'a liberal democracy'.

- Periods and events: the Middle Ages, the First World War.
- Geographical names if they are part of the title of an area or country: South Dakota, Western Australia, Norfolk Broads but not 'the west of Scotland'.
- Trade names such as Formica, Perspex, Thermos. These proprietary names must be capitalised as their proprietors insist on it. Also use capitals for makes of car, aircraft, etc.
- Book, journal and article titles: these are covered in the section on references, pp.44–50.
- References in the text to figures, tables, etc.

Cross-references

A properly cross-referenced text is very helpful to the reader, particularly if time or budget does not permit you to have an index. The author may have already provided extensive cross-references in the typescript, using the relevant page numbers of the typescript. Before you send the typescript off for setting, all these cross-references should be changed to the figures 00, if they are to single pages, or to 00–00 or 00ff (depending on the style adopted) if they are to multiple pages, as the page numbers of the work when typeset will differ from the page numbers of the typescript. However, do not obliterate or white-out the page numbers which the author has so painstakingly inserted since you – or the author – will find it much easier to insert the new numbers on the page proof if you can turn up the correct section of text by looking back at the typescript.

The reason for inserting the blank figures 00 is so that the right amount of space for the actual page numbers can be left by the typesetter in each line. This makes for speedier and cheaper correction on the page proofs.

If the book's paragraphs or sections are numbered then cross-references to these can be done on the typescript, and will only have to be altered if there are changes to the numbering sequence at a later stage.

Dates and Time

The simplest style for these is best: 4 January, 4 January 1950, January 1950. Decades are best expressed in full (the 1970s, not 1970's or '70s) or, if you are certain there will be no confusion, the seventies (not the 'seventies). Centuries are spelt out: the eighteenth century (adjective: eighteenth-century). The use of a hyphen in mid-eighteenth century looks better than mid eighteenth century, although technically there is no such century.

Pairs of dates are usually expressed in the shortest pronounceable form (1971–4, 1914–18, 1837–1901) when they appear in text. But they are usually left in full when they appear in display setting. The dash between the two dates is an unspaced en dash (for explanation of the kinds of dashes, see pp.38–9)

When describing a length of time between two years, use the word 'to' rather than a dash: 'the campaign lasted from 1979 to 1981' not 'from 1979–81'.

Sentences should not start with a figure, so one that starts with a year may need to be rewritten.

Italic and Roman Type

Matter that is to be set in italic (sloping) type is underlined in the text. Upright type is usually called roman. If you get the opportunity, try to make your author leave as much copy as possible non-underlined, since it is very time-consuming going through the text deleting underlining from material which is not to be set in italic type (such as quoted material, which some typists are taught to underline).

In general italic is used for:

* Book titles, except for the Bible, its constituent books and the Koran. Titles of chapters, articles and unpublished words are set in roman inside quotes.
* Titles of periodicals and newspapers. The usual convention is that the word 'The' is italicised only in the title of *The Times* and *The Economist.*
* Titles of films, plays, works of art, long poems, pieces of music given descriptive titles by the composer. Nicknames to pieces of music (Beethoven's 'Pastoral' Symphony) and names of songs ('Pennies from Heaven') are in roman with quotes. Unadorned titles for music (Symphony No 41 in F major) are set in roman without quotes.
* Names of ships are set in italic but prefixes, such as HMS or SS, are set in roman.
* Names of parties in legal cases are set in italic. The letter v. between them is set in roman.
* Foreign words or phrases that have not yet been incorporated into English. Words that have been incorporated into English are set in roman. The distinction between these may be somewhat arbitrary: *Hart's Rules*, for instance, would italicise *coup d'état* but leave 'chargé d'affaires' in roman. This is definitely a matter for your decision and then your running style sheet, or you can follow the guidance in *Hart's Rules* and *The Oxford Dictionary for Writers and Editors.*

Roman type is used for:

* House, pub and hotel names and all the common abbreviations such as cf., e.g., i.e., etc.
* Titles of chapters in books, articles in periodicals, short poems and short extracts from text are set in roman type in quotation marks:

In their chapter 'Arrest and interrogation procedures' in *Your Rights and the Law*, Upboyze and Attam insist that 'detained persons should always be polite to the police'.

Lists

Lists in the text can present a number of problems. Two types of list may be found. The first is the tabloid newspaper style list, where each item is preceded by a typographic device such as a bullet point, an asterisk or a dash. With newspaper writers list-mania can reach absurd proportions. Keith Waterhouse, in *Waterhouse on Newspaper Style*, describes it as a neurosis: 'They cannot stop themselves arranging pieces of copy to resemble mail-order catalogues or railway timetables. They do it on the slightest excuse, leaping on any combination of words that ... can be passed off as tabulation.'[2] He recommends, for newspapers, that typographical signposts should only be used when the list or catalogue is a genuine one, not just to 'jolly up' the text. This recommendation applies equally to books and pamphlets.

There is a second type of list commonly found in books. This is where subsidiary points are made in the forms of numbered or lettered subsections. The beginning and end of each subsection needs to be made clear. This is usually done by indenting the subsections, similarly to the treatment of quoted material (see p.40). It is also possible to use 'hanging indentation', with the first line full out to the left margin and subsequent 'turned over' lines indented. This has been used in the Glossary in this book, see pp.154–61. If the numbering or lettering sequence covers more than one paragraph and it is essential to show where the sequence ends, then this is the clearest method to use.

There are also two possible styles of indentation and these need to be checked for consistency. These are:

(a) XXXXXXXXXXX   (a) XXXXXXXXXX
    XXXXXXXXXXX   XXXXXXXXXXXX

A line space should precede and follow any indented sequence and the first paragraph of the following copy should be full out.

The usual numbering and lettering sequence, where there are sections, subsections and sub-subsections, is 1., 2., 3. (a), (b), (c); (i), (ii), (iii). If you have any further sections then your text is almost certainly too complicated! To avoid confusion with any letters or numbers in the text it is better in lists to use Arabic numbers followed by a full point, or letters or Roman numerals in parentheses.

Follow a consistent style over the use of capitals or lower-case at the beginning of items in lists, and punctuation marks such as full points or semi-colons at the end.

Numbers

In general books, that is not scientific or technical books, the usual rule is that numbers up to and including ten are spelled out. Numbers over 11, or numbers under 11 used with larger numbers, are expressed in figures: 'the crowd swelled from 10 to 30'. Indefinite numbers are usually spelled out: 'about a thousand times'.

Sentences should not begin with a figure; they should be written out in full or the sentence should be rephrased.

Figures should be used for exact measurements attached to units ('ten children' but '50 kg') and for cross-references ('see Chapter 6'). Percentages are often expressed in figures, since this is essential if they contain a part of a full unit ('6.5 per cent'), although they may look better spelled out if the work is more general ('the proportion varied between five and ten per cent').

In thousands be consistent in the use of commas. It is quite common for them only to be used for numbers greater than either 2,000 or 10,000. Numbers in millions are better as '6 million' rather than 6,000,000; 6 m may be confusing since the abbreviation 'm' is still occasionally used for thousands.

The use of numbers follows the same rules as dates: they are 'elided' with an unspaced en dash so that as few figures as possible are used. So, 26–8, 144–65, 288–309. An exception is often made for the numbers 11 to 19 in each hundred, which retain the 'tens' figure : 211–15. When numbers are elided, check that the sense is correct: 2–3,000 or 2,000–3,000. If there is any ambiguity then use the numbers in full.

Punctuation

Whole books are written about punctuation. Not surprisingly, perhaps, when its incorrect use can alter completely what someone is trying to say. This section deals only with some particular points which concern the copy-editor. For general rules, consult a more detailed work, such as *Mind the Stop* by G.V. Carey (see the Further Reading section, pp.150–3).

Rules and Hyphens Most typesetting systems and some DTP programs have two kinds of dash or rule and a hyphen available, whereas a typewriter just has a hyphen. Thus it is usually necessary for the copy-editor to mark the copy to show which kind is required if there is likely to be any confusion.

Of the two kinds of rule the shorter is the en rule (so called because it is one en wide: see p.73 for definition of en and em). This has two main functions. The first is to replace the word 'and' or 'to' as in the 'London–Glasgow train', '1914–18 war'. There is usually no space between the rule and the words or figures it joins.

The second function of the en rule is as the parenthetical dash. Here space is left on each side, and, if this is not left on the copy, a vertical line should be marked to show the typesetter that a space should be left. 'The influence of three painters – Manet, Monet and Cézanne – can be clearly seen.'

To indicate to the typesetter that an en rule should be used rather than hyphen, write the word 'en' or the letter 'N' above the typewritten dash.

The longer em rule is used to indicate the omission of a word or part of a word. It may also be used as a parenthetical dash, though this is less common. It is more often used in indexes and bibliographies to stand for a repeated name. (Sometimes a double em rule is used for this.)

Thomas, Dylan, 17, 28, 56–8
— and Vernon Watkins, correspondence, 93–5, 102

It may also be used in tables to mark a blank entry and instead of asterisks or bullets in lists (but see p.37).

The hyphenation and joining of compound words can cause a number of problems if the text is not consistent. *Hart's Rules* and *The Oxford Dictionary for Writers and Editors* give guidance over which words should be hyphenated, joined up or just left separate. It is often a matter of taste. Note, however, a common error, which is to hyphenate a construction such as long-term or up-to-date when it is used as a predicate. These should be hyphenated only when they are used attributively: 'These are the most up-to-date records. The records are not up to date.'

Parentheses and Brackets Typesetters call ( ) parentheses and [ ] brackets. Longer brackets used to group items in a table are called braces.

Square brackets have one common function in general books, which is to indicate words inserted by the author in quoted material to clarify or query the meaning. For example, 'it was well known that John [Brown] had a vile temper.' They also have a specialist use in legal references (see pp.48–50).

Apostrophes Whether an extra 's' is added after an apostrophe in the possessive case of words ending in 's' is usually decided on what sounds best. *Hart's Rules* recommends adding 's to all one and two syllable words and longer words spoken with stress on the penultimate syllable, such as James's, Dickens's and Zacharias's.

Watch out for incorrect apostrophes in it's and its, yours, hers, theirs, etc.

Apostrophes are not necessary in plurals such as 1960s and MPs, but they may be necessary in special cases like 'dotting i's and crossing t's'.

Common Punctuation Faults Typists are often taught habits which are not followed in printed books. Among the conventions of which they may not be aware are the following:

- There is no comma before an opening parenthesis.
- A full point comes before the closing parenthesis if the whole sentence is in parentheses: otherwise it comes after the closing parenthesis. For example:

    Jane insisted on rewriting the essay. (Ruth had encountered her stubbornness before.)
    Jane looked curiously at Ruth (who had taken off her coat and placed it on the chair).

- There is no need for double punctuation at the end of a sentence after an abbreviation or a punctuation mark which appears inside quotes.
- There should be no full points at the end of items in a list of illustrations, etc., or at the end of headings.
- A colon introducing a list or other displayed material should not be followed by a dash.

Quoted Matter
Prose quotations should be broken off from the text if they are more than a few lines in length (usually about five lines). Shorter quotations can be broken off if the context demands it, for example if they need to be set out as examples or specimens, or if they are lines of verse. If they are woven into the text then quotation marks are used. The usual style of most UK publishers is to use single quotation marks, and double for quotes inside quotes.

Quoted matter separated from the rest of the text can be treated in a number of different ways. This will be covered under design of the text, see p.85. But however it is dealt with, it is usual for quoted material to be set apart from the text by a line space above and below. The first line of the copy which follows it is therefore set full out and not indented. Usually it is not surrounded by quotation marks.

Spelling
Good spelling is an essential skill for the copy-editor. A good dictionary is vital and a consistent style within the text should be followed. A few points to watch out for include:

- A number of words have alternative spellings in common use, such as despatch/dispatch, gipsy/gypsy. (Sometimes the American alternative spelling creeps into UK authors' text.)
- The suffixes -ise and -ize are often alternative correct spellings. You should make a decision as to whether to use -ise or -ize endings. However some words can only take -ise, such as improvise, supervise, televise.
- Some words, such as dependent (adjective)/dependant (noun) have alternative spellings depending on which part of speech they are.
- Some words, such as principle/principal and forego/forgo have different meanings depending on which way they are spelled.

How far you should go in correcting spelling, etc. in quoted material from other sources is always debatable. You may choose, for instance, to retain American spelling.

Subheadings
In most short books, two 'grades' of subheadings should be sufficient. In a longer book, three are permissible. Authors who want more grades than three should be discouraged. If the author has numbered the sections, then consider whether this is necessary (although it has advantages for both cross-referencing and indexing). The levels of subheadings should be marked with a code, usually a pencil capital letter A, B, or C in a square. The subheadings should be checked for consistency in capitalisation, etc. and should not end in a full point. Design of subheadings is covered on p.85.

Style and Solecisms
Copy-editors sometimes develop a taste for nit-picking at an individual author's style of writing. There is a vogue nowadays for being ultra-pedantic, with the use of language becoming the object of debate in the serious press. This has not gone unnoticed among those who think language must evolve and that rearguard actions against, say, split infinitives or the word 'hopefully' serve only to stifle the natural development of the tongue. One American writer, Jim Quinn, recently attacked those 'professional busybodies and righters of imaginary wrongs [who] are the Sunday visitors of language, dropping in weekly on the local paper to make sure that everything is up to their idea of standard.'[3]

The good copy-editor should be trying to remove the author's *solecisms* (incorrect grammar or idiom) but retain her or his individual *style*. The line between the two may be narrow. For instance, most authorities agree that the rhythm of a sentence may require an infinitive to be split. 'To boldly go' may sound better than 'boldly to go', or 'to go boldly'. Even so, like me, you might still want to try to recast such constructions. You may not succeed.

A number of useful books on style are listed in the Further Reading section (pp.150–3).

Equal Opportunities in Print

Traditional guides to style have a traditional fault – they take no position on prejudice in language and in books.[4] Those who compiled them would doubtless never consider themselves racist or sexist but the guides they have produced often do not recognise language which is prejudiced in terms of sex, race, sexuality, age or disability. There is deep, institutional discrimination in our society against women, black and other ethnic minority people, lesbians and gay men, people with disabilities and older and younger people. This has to be combatted positively, not ignored.

The users of English, the Western world's most common language, have a particular responsibility. For as the language has spread and been enriched by contact with people from different cultures, it has become more necessary to rid it of the bias it has unconsciously acquired. The word 'black', for instance, is often used in a pejorative way:

> She felt a mood of black despair.
> The unions have blacked this factory.

Without being over-pedantic, it is possible to take some steps to redress the balance. This is certainly the view of the National Union of Journalists Book Branch, to which many book editors and production staff belong:

> Those of us who earn our living in book publishing – whether by commissioning, editing, illustrating, designing, producing, presenting or selling books – have a professional and social obligation to use words, phrases and images that do not reinforce offensive or discriminatory attitudes ... It is up to us to join with those outside the publishing industry in the effort to eradicate such words, phrases and long-established habits of communication and thereby take part in changing the attitudes which they reflect and reinforce.[5]

It is not practical in a short book of this kind to go into great detail about how discrimination and prejudice in writing can be removed. A small number of books and pamphlets do exist and some of these are listed in the Further Reading section (see pp.150–3.) There are, however, three main areas in which judicious editing can go some way towards producing 'equal opportunity copy'. Briefly, they are as follows.

Elimination of Prejudiced Vocabulary It is often possible, for instance, to use words which are not derived from the word 'man'. So use 'people' rather than 'mankind', 'artificial' rather than 'manmade', 'predecessors' or 'forebears' rather than 'forefathers'. Work titles are often sexist and can be changed; use 'firefighter' rather than 'fireman'; 'refuse collector' rather than 'dustman'.

Female versions of otherwise non-sex specific work titles are not necessary: conductress, actress, air hostess.

'They', 'she or he' or 's/he' can all be used instead of 'he' when the sex of the person being discussed is unknown.

Descriptions, Characters and Interests Women and men, black people and white, should all be described as people, not stereotypes. Women are not more emotional, sentimental, vain, fickle or weak than men. Men are not dominating, more sensible or superior. Black and other ethnic community people should not be characterised in terms of their race.

Social Stereotyping Not everyone lives in a nuclear family. In fact only about 10 per cent of the UK population live in circumstances where a man is the sole breadwinner for a family of a wife and children. Nor is everyone heterosexual or without disability. Copy should not be allowed to reflect this without challenge.

Positive Images You may want to take a more positive stand on equal opportunities than just 'editing-out', as set out above. A process of 'writing in' can be used to promote positive images of women, black and other ethnic community people, lesbians and gay men, older and younger people and people with disabilities. You will almost certainly want to involve the author in any such changes you make to the text.

Rather than providing specific guidelines it is useful to ask yourself a set of questions when assessing any text or illustration. A checklist could include questions similar to these:

- Is it non-sexist or positively anti-sexist?
- Is it non-racist or positively anti-racist?
- Does it positively promote anti-heterosexism, anti-ageism and anti-ablebodiedism?
- Does it, in general, promote action against discrimination and oppression, besides pointing out where it exists?
- Does it rely on stereotype or tokenism in its attempts to make its anti-discriminatory points?
- Does it implicitly assume that the reader is a white, heterosexual, able-bodied male?

Preparing the End Matter

The material which appears after the text is known collectively as the end matter. In a short pamphlet no one may have thought of the need for such matter and so none may have been provided when the typescript arrives with you. However, you may feel that the finished product will be improved by the addition of, for example, a glossary, a bibliography or an index. You may well find, in this case, that you are left to provide these. If that is so, you should find the following section useful. It should also be useful for you if you have to turn whatever material you have been provided with into a useful source of information for the reader.

Appendices

Appendices usually come first of all in the end matter, directly after the text. Their purpose is to set out in full material which is relevant but too long or diversionary to appear in the body of the text (and to save space). If there are a number of appendices then they can be run on, rather than each starting on a new page. It is usually sufficient for the heading to be the word 'Appendix' (or 'Appendices') and not the actual title of the appendix. This can be set instead in the heaviest of the weights used for subheadings (see p.41).

Bibliographies and References

You may not think that your book needs references, in the formal sense, where the source of each piece of information is identified. But it is quite likely that your authors drew on already published work and this at least should be identified, so that others' work is acknowledged and readers can follow up anything that interests them. You might even want to guide them in their researches by including a 'further reading' section.

If you want to identify specifically the sources of information, then you do this by inserting an indicator (either a superscript number, such as [1][2][3], or a symbol such as an asterisk) at a relevant point in the text. This points the reader to a note elsewhere where a reference is given, in a standard form. These, obviously, follow the order in which they fall in the book. If the references are further compiled into another list, to be printed in the book, it can be called a number of things. A list called 'references' or 'works cited' should contain only the works cited in the text and no other. If it contains either more or less than the references then it is called a 'bibliography'. If it is very many less than the references then it should be called a 'select bibliography'. A more informal list, which does not contain specific notes on the text, is usually called 'further reading'. Sometimes the list is presented not in a dispassionate academic style but in a more opinionated form where the author's comments on the sources are included. This is usually called a bibliography, although this is not an accurate definition.

Bibliographies, reading lists and references can be a real headache for the copy-editor if they are not properly prepared, so you would be well advised to communicate with your authors at an early stage to ensure they produce the material in the correct form.

As with everything else, what you are aiming for is consistency. But although there are rules and systems, some of which are described below, if your authors have produced a consistent, logical and unambiguous list then you should consider whether it is worth all the effort of changing it to turn it into your own preferred style.

Some people – mainly academics – make rather a fetish of referencing and insist on providing sources for every morsel of information they have included. Gentle persuasion may be necessary to get them to change, so that the text is clearer for the general reader.

Footnotes or Endnotes If there is just a smattering of notes in the text (say one or two, every few pages) then it is perfectly possible, and probably desirable for the reader, to set them as footnotes at the bottom of the relevant page. You can use either superscript numbers or symbols to mark the note in the text and you repeat the number or symbol at the bottom of the page followed by the reference. The accepted order of symbols used is * † ‡ ¶ and you start the sequence again on a fresh page of text. If you have more than this number of notes in a sequence you can either start the numbers again on the following page, or run the sequence throughout the whole chapter or the whole book. The text for footnotes can be typed at the bottom of the relevant page of the typescript. It should appear on the same galley proof as the text, set in the correct size, and the typesetter's attention drawn to it when the proofs are passed, so that it is correctly placed when the pages are 'made up'. For more about how typesetting is made up into pages, see pp.111–13.

If there are more than a few references then you will probably need to have them as endnotes either at the end of each chapter or the end of the book as a whole. Which you do is debatable. Readers probably find it easier to turn to references at the end of chapters and there is no particular saving on cost in putting them all to the end of the book. There can be a saving on time, however, since you can pass the galley proofs of the text back to the printer to be made up into pages while you are still correcting the references. With endnotes you need to use a numbering sequence for the identifiers. It is more usual to start the sequence again at the beginning of each chapter, if only so that you do not need to alter the whole sequence if a note is added or deleted at some point in the editing or production process. The text for endnotes should be typed on separate pages from the rest of the text.

Whichever system you use, you should try to avoid notes which are mini-essays on related topics. This quirky habit persists amongst some authors who probably see themselves as latter-day Laurence Sternes or Karl Marxes.

The Short-title Reference System The most useful system of referencing for the small publisher is undoubtedly the short-title system. This is the system most commonly used in what publishers and academics call the humanities. Scientific publishers often use other systems, particularly the author-date (Harvard) system. These are not described here, but full descriptions can be found in other more specialised works such as *Copy-editing* by Judith Butcher and the *Chicago Manual of Style*.

The short-title system works by giving a full reference only at the first mention in the book. If there are a lot of references, then an alternative is to give a full reference at the first mention in each chapter.

The first reference to a book should be in the following form:

1. Author's name. Full forenames can be used, or just initials, but whichever style is adopted should be used throughout.
2. Book title, underlined for italic type except for unpublished work or manuscripts (which should be set in roman type and enclosed by quote marks).
3. Editor, compiler or translator, if any. This appears as the first item if there is no author.
4. Series name and number in series, if any.
5. Edition, if not the first.
6. Number of volumes, publication place, publisher and date, all in parentheses.
7. Volume (if more than one) and page number (if appropriate).

This can be shortened by omitting the publisher and even the publication place, particularly in a short non-academic book, since librarians do not use this information for cataloguing purposes and it may not greatly help the reader to locate the source. However, many people undoubtedly find it useful for tracing older or more obscure material, so you should consider it carefully before leaving it out.

Two examples of correctly written references are thus:

Simon Snodgrass, *My Life and Experiences in the Fish-canning Industry*, 3rd edn (London, Boring and Dull, 1953), p.123.
Jane Whitewell, *The Highways and Byways of Penge*, ed. Arthur Vernon, Backstreets of London series, vol. 8 (Oxford, Obscure and Obscure, 1983), p.456.

Subsequent references to a book should contain the author's surname, a shortened version of the title, and the volume and page number. The two examples above would become:

Snodgrass, *Fish-canning*, p.175.
Whitewell, *Penge*, vol.8, p.222.

This system means that the abbreviation *op. cit.* is not used. This was the traditional reference to a source already cited. The use of a short title is preferable since the reference is immediately more identifiable when the reader turns up the note and it allows for the fact that there may be references to more than one book by the same author. The reference *ibid.* (which means 'in the same place') can be used if there are two or more consecutive notes to the same volume, although for the sake of unambiguity a short title may be preferable.

References to articles in multi-author books and specialist journals are given in the following form:

1. Author's name.
2. Article title, not underlined (roman type), with single quote marks.
3. The title of the journal or the book, underlined for italic type.
4. Editor(s) name(s), for a multi-author book; but do not list the editor for a journal.
5. Volume number, if there is one, and date, for a journal.
6. Publication place, publisher and date, all in parentheses for a multi-author book.
7. Page number.

Second and subsequent references are given by shortening the title of the article.

Thus examples of correctly written references are as follows:

Vera Turgid, 'Significance of Writer's Cramp Symptoms in the Work of Tolstoy', *Journal of Obscure Literary Research,* vol.15, no.3, p.76.
G. Kelly and F. Astaire, 'Dancing in the Dark' in *Tripping the Light Fantastic,* ed. C. Charisse (New York, Pirouette Press, 1958), p.123.

References to newspapers and non-specialist periodicals do not require the title of the article, the author or the page number. All that is required is the title of the newspaper or periodical and the date:

The Times, 22 February 1984.
New Statesman, 13 March 1981.
Daily Mirror, 16 April 1962.

The correct titles of the verbatim records of parliamentary proceedings are House of Commons Debates and House of Lords Debates. However, they are commonly called *Hansard*, after the man who pioneered the taking of a shorthand record. It is usually quite sufficient to give the reference in the form:

Hansard, 15 February 1984, col.123.

for House of Commons debates and:

Hansard (House of Lords), 16 March 1985, col.456.

for those in the Lords.

Note that Written Answers provided by ministers (in both houses of parliament) are numbered with separate column numbers and so should be distinguished by including the words 'Written Answer' or the abbreviation 'WA' in the reference. Committee proceedings are also recorded verbatim and if the reference is to one of these then this should also be made clear.

Official publications by the UK government, civil service departments and some quangos are often published by Her Majesty's Stationery Office (HMSO). It is usually best for these to be referenced under the name of the department or body which produced them, since this will be more useful to your readers. However, in the case of some types of report, such as that of a Royal Commission, for instance, it is better to reference them under the name of that commission, since that is how they are usually known. General rules in these cases are hard to make, and provided a consistent approach is taken then accurate referencing can be imposed.

Many, but not all, official publications contain a 'Command number' which appears on the title page and is preceded by the prefix C, Cd, Cmd, Cmnd or Cm. These different abbreviations all refer to different series of papers and should not be altered. The present series use the prefix Cm, which started in 1987, so any recent paper should have this prefix. Be warned, however, that HMSO in Edinburgh and Belfast have separate sequences of Command numbers and are still using the older abbreviations, so if the paper has come from either the Scottish Office or the Northern Ireland Office then it may be deceptive.

Publications of the House of Commons and the House of Lords, such as reports by select committees, are numbered with the prefix HC and HL respectively. A new numbering system starts with every parliamentary session and so both the dates of the session and the number should be included within the reference. For example:

Statement of Change in Immigration Rules, HC (1980–1) No. 84.

Small Publishing Co-op
456 Worthy Road
London N29 9KL

References

The short title system for references should
be used, as shown in the following examples.

1. Rita Jones, <u>Landlord and Tenant Law</u>, 3rd
edn (London, Legal and Eagle, 1988) p.123.

2. James Smith, 'Recent changes in tenants'
rights', <u>Housing Rights Journal</u>, Autumn 1989,
p.37.

3. Department of the Environment, <u>Housing:</u>
<u>the Government's proposals</u>, Cm 214 (London,
HMSO, 1987) p.43.

4. Commission for Racial Equality, <u>A Guide</u>
<u>for Accommodation Agencies and Landlords</u>
(London, CRE, 1982) p.43.

5. Jones, <u>Landlord and Tenant Law</u>, p.234.

6. Jones, <u>Landlord and Tenant Law</u>, p.252.

7. <u>The Times</u>, 4 January 1989.

8. <u>Hansard</u>, 13 December 1988, col. 78 (WA).

9. CRE, <u>Accommodation Agencies and Landlords</u>,
p.22.

Figure 4.5. Correctly typed list of references.

References: Summary Because the preparation of references can be such a headache it can be useful if you prepare a sample of how you would like your authors to present them. This can be attached to your list of points to send to authors before they start writing their text (see p.19). An example of such a list can be seen in Figure 4.5, p.49.

Legal references and Acts of Parliament In recent years, the law has come to play a more important role in ordinary life in Britain as political decisions are frequently challenged in the courts. Small publishers therefore often find themselves commenting on legal issues and it may be helpful to summarise here a few of the principles involved in referring to legal cases, so that your text becomes even more useful to those whose job it is to interpret – and change – the law.

References to cases are given in the form *Patel* v. *Jones*, with the name of the plaintiff and defendant in italic and the v. (standing for versus) in roman. In general books, it may be enough just to cite the year the case occurred, in parentheses. But if the case is unusual, or you want to help lawyers and others find a specialised reference, then you should set out the reference to the law report in which the case appears, in the way described below.

Law reports are generally called by the name of the court in which they appeared (such as AC for Appeal Court or HL for House of Lords) or by the name of the series in which they are published, such as All ER (All England Law Reports). These are numbered in different ways, depending on how many volumes are published in any year. Where there is one volume per year, and the year forms the number of the volume, the year is given in square brackets, in the form [1962] AC 209. Where there are several volumes per year, the year is given in brackets followed by the volume number within that year, for example: [1978] 2 All ER 456. Where the volumes are numbered separately from the year, or in cases reported in the non-specialist press, the year is given in parentheses before the volume or date, for example: (1987) The Times 23 November 1987. (Note that italic is not used for the names of reports or journals, that page numbers are not prefixed by p., and that it is important to follow the standard practice on use of brackets [ ] and parentheses ( ).)

Acts of Parliament (usually called statutes in legal books) should be given their full name and year at the first mention in the text (note that there is no comma between the title of the Act and the calendar year it was passed). References to parts of an Act should use the system of sections, subsections, paragraphs and subparagraphs used in the Act itself. This can get very complicated, for example: Representation of the People Act 1949, s. 63 (1) (*c*) (i).

Bibliography

The differences between a bibliography and a 'further reading' list are discussed above (see p.44). If the author has already provided one then this should be checked against the references, so that the style of entry is consistent with the system used there. If the bibliography is supposed to be a complete list of all the works cited in the text, it is useful to check off each entry in it on a photocopy as you go through the text doing your detailed copy-editing. That way you will pick up any missing items.

Bibliographies themselves can be listed in a number of ways. They can be strictly alphabetical or they can be categorised in some way to make points about the text. This can be either by subject matter, or by the kind of sources used (such as manuscript material and published material). If your author has categorised the bibliography in some way then she or he is likely to have strong views if you change it. Providing it is consistent within itself and with references, there is little point in doing so.

Glossary

If a glossary is necessary then it should be checked against the text for spelling etc. You should also note, while copy-editing the text, any words which seem unfamiliar to you which the author has not included, and check with him or her whether they should be added.

Glossaries set in single column are generally laid out as a 'hanging indent', with the key word set full out in italic type and turned lines indented.

Index

If your book needs an index – and virtually every non-fiction book is made more useful when one is included – then you should consider employing a specialist indexer. A complex book is always better for having a properly compiled index, and it is not a job that an inexperienced person can undertake. However, you may have inserted the requirement to produce an index in your author's contract.

A list of members of the Society of Indexers is available from the Society, whose address is given in the Useful Organisations list, p.149.

If you do not wish to employ a specialist, and your author is unwilling or unable to do so, then you have little option but to compile the index yourself.

For most books, an index can only be compiled when the book is at the page proof stage, since only then will the pages on which individual subject entries fall be known. An exception can be made if a book has paragraph numbers, and the index is compiled from these. This can save a little time at the later stages of a book's production.

Indexes are often still compiled by hand on cards or slips of paper, although the advent of the word processor and the computer has made some of the routine work more easy to handle. Word-search programs can be used but they inevitably throw up every mention of an entry. The skill of the human indexer is in deciding what should be indexed and how.

A very full explanation of how to comb through a set of page proofs, make up cards and type up and present the text is to be found in the *Chicago Manual of Style* (see the Further Reading section, pp. 150–3).

Index definitions An index is a series of alphabetically organised sign-posts to items in a book, which has itself been organised according to some other scheme.

A simple index contains a heading and one or more page references. A complex entry contains a heading and sub-entries and sometimes sub-sub-entries). For example:

Typography 27, 42
   Books 45
   Historical background 43
   Magazines 47, 50

Sub-entries may start on a fresh line (as here) or run on, separated by semi-colons.

Compilation The British Standard, BS 3700: *Preparation of Indexes*, recommends that 'main headings should normally be nouns (qualified or unqualified) rather than adjectives or verbs on their own.' If adjectives have been used then the heading should never be used as noun and adjective in the same entry, for example:

Child
   Pre-school
   Labour

Judith Butcher in *Copy-editing* recommends that entries containing more than six references and references spanning more than nine pages should be broken down into sub-entries.

When words are used in more than one form in the text (for example in both singular and plural) then only one form should be used in the index. Words with different meanings under different contexts should be indexed separately.

Alphabetical order can either be word by word or letter by letter, and should be consistently one or the other. In each case, letters are only counted up to the first comma or other punctuation mark. In word by word order, short words precede longer words beginning with the same letters and hyphenated words are usually counted as two words unless part is a prefix or suffix which cannot stand alone.

Word by word	Letter by letter
Pay as you earn	Pay as you earn
Pay statement	PAYE, see Pay as you earn
PAYE, see Pay as you earn	Payment in lieu
Payment in lieu	Pay statement

In word by word order, sub-entries may be in the order of the most significant word, rather than strictly alphabetical.

Style Within the Entry In general, keep capitalisation, wording and punctuation to a minimum. Sub-entries may be run on to save space, and the convention is that they are then separated by semi-colons. Turned over lines are usually then indented. Page numbers should be 'elided', so that as few figures as possible are used (see p.38.) Bold or italic type can be used to distinguish important references from more casual ones.

Unjustified typesetting is preferable, since it reduces unsightly wordbreaks and wordspacing.

'Advertisement' or Further Information

It is often the case that the last two or three pages of a book or pamphlet are empty, since books usually have to be printed in multiples of at least four pages. These spare pages can be used for publicity for other books or pamphlets you have produced, or for your organisation. Because people are often reluctant to cut pages from anything which has got information on the reverse you should ensure that something like a reply coupon or membership form is backed up with a blank page. As you may not know until a late stage that you are going to have some blank pages at the back of the book (because, for example, the index copy only arrives at the last moment), then you may have to make a quick decision about what copy to put there. With this in mind, it is very useful to have some 'instant copy' or better still, instant artwork, which you can put on this page. If your organisation does not have a membership form or publicity leaflet of the right size then perhaps you should get one designed and ready for action.

Preparing the Figurative Matter

Figures and tables require different treatment from the rest of the text and it is therefore convenient to discuss them altogether in one section.

Table 6: Unemployment change in five London boroughs between 1979 and 1986.

	October 1979		March 1986		Change 1979-86	
	No.	%	No.	%	No.	%
UK	1,206,000	4.6	3,199,400	11.9	1,993,400	165.3
Greater London						
Camden	4,024	3.8	15,389	15.9	11,365	282.4
Greenwich	4,065	3.8	14,792	13.8	10,727	263.9
Hackney	5,258	5.7	20,527	22.3	15,269	290.4
Haringey	4,491	4.1	17,501	16.8	13,010	289.7
Islington	5,244	6.0	16,735	19.2	11,491	219.1
Five borough total	23,082	4.7	85,304	17.8	61,862	266.8

Source: Department of Employment

Table 6: Unemployment change in five London boroughs between 1979 and 1986

	October 1979		*March 1986*		*Change 1979-86*	
	No.	*%*	*No.*	*%*	*No.*	*%*
UK	1,206,000	4.6	3,199,400	11.9	1,993,400	165.3
Greater London						
Camden	4,024	3.8	15,389	15.9	11,365	282.4
Greenwich	4,065	3.8	14,792	13.8	10,727	263.9
Hackney	5,258	5.7	20,527	22.3	15,269	290.4
Haringey	4,491	4.1	17,501	16.8	13,010	289.7
Islington	5,244	6.0	16,735	19.2	11,491	219.1
Five borough total	23,082	4.7	85,304	17.8	61,862	266.8

Source: Department of Employment

Figure 4.6. Table in typescript (reduced) and its printed version.
To make it fit, the typist had to type the table in landscape shape, whereas when typeset it will fit comfortably into a portrait shaped page, set in 8pt type.

For the sake of ease of reference, a single numbering sequence for all figurative matter is preferable, although authors may prefer to have tables and figures numbered separately.

It may not be possible to put the figures and tables in the printed book exactly where they fall in the typescript, since the pagination will not be the same. The copy should be checked and references in it to 'see the following figure', for example, changed to 'see Figure 00'.

A note should be written in the margin of the relevant portion of the typescript saying 'Figure 00 near here' so that it can be positioned as accurately as possible when the type is being made up into pages.

Figures
These can be defined as material which is set apart from the text for some reason. They can be diagrams or other illustrative material such as newspaper cuttings or, as is the case in this book, specimens of schedules, instruction sheets or type.

You may have been provided with diagrams which are ready to be reproduced (what is known as 'camera-ready artwork'.) Perhaps more likely is that you will have got a mishmash of material which has to be made reproducible. How you do this is discussed in Chapter 6, on pp.117–21.

Tables
Clearly typed and laid out tables are a boon to the designer and typesetter and so you should take some time making sure they are in a good condition. A specimen of a well-typed and presented table is shown in Figure 4.6, opposite. It is worth getting all tables in a text retyped if there are major inconsistencies.

It is not necessary for you to work out the exact spacing of the columns: this can be left to the designer and typesetter. What you should do is make sure that there is no inconsistency or ambiguity in the typing. For instance, there may be confusion if there are two levels of column heading. If so a pencilled bracket should be drawn on the typescript to indicate exactly what a heading refers to.

All tables should have a heading and these should be checked throughout the typescript for consistency. Parallel tables should be laid out in similar ways (they might not be if they have been compiled by different people or they come from different sources). Units should always be stated, either in the main headings or above the relevant column. Vertical rules are nearly always unnecessary but you do not need to delete them on the typescript as this can be covered by the designer's mark-up. You should check for alignment of decimal points and consistency in the number of decimal places. Avoid ditto marks by repeating information or using subheadings. All tables should be given sources and the same style as for references should be used.

Sources

This entire chapter owes an incalculable debt to Judith Butcher, *Copy-editing: The Cambridge Handbook*, 3rd edition (Cambridge, Cambridge University Press, 1992). In many ways, this book was inspired by Ms Butcher's example, which is all a manual of instruction should be: lucid, comprehensive, full of common sense, and written with respect for its subject.

Two further guides to publishers' style were also very useful. *The Chicago Manual of Style*, 13th edition (Chicago, University of Chicago Press, 1982) is impressively comprehensive. *Hart's Rules for Compositors and Readers at the University Press, Oxford*, 39th edition (Oxford, Oxford University Press, 1983) is slim, but often helpful.

References

1.   Defined in P.G. Burbidge, *Prelims and End Pages* (Cambridge, Cambridge University Press, 1969).
2.   Keith Waterhouse, *Waterhouse on Newspaper Style* (London, Viking, 1989).
3.   Jim Quinn, *American Tongue in Cheek*. Cited in Bill Bryson, *The Penguin Dictionary of Troublesome Words* (Harmondsworth, Penguin, 1984).
4.   The latest edition of Sir Ernest Gowers, *The Complete Plain Words*, 3rd edition revised by Sidney Greenbaum and Janet Whitcut (London, HMSO, 1986) takes some recognisance of sexism in language. Judith Butcher in *Copy-editing*, 3rd edition, goes a lot further than this and discusses positive ways of removing bias.
5.   National Union of Journalists Book Branch, *Non-sexist Code of Practice for Book Publishing* (London, NUJ, 1982).

5
Design

Introduction

The first chapters of this book dealt with how to produce a complete
and consistent text. This one will discuss how to combine the text and
illustrations in a simple and attractive way. This chapter is not, however,
a complete graphic design course. Design can only be learned by
practice, either at college or in on-the-job training. What this chapter
attempts is to set out some important principles which underlie good
design when applied to book production and to outline some simple
techniques which can be used in the production of a straightforward
book or pamphlet. The creative flair, that extra spark which turns a
run-of-the-mill but slightly boring job into a fine piece of work, can
only come from you.

You may wonder why it is necessary to get your job designed at all.
Surely it would be simpler just to hand the whole thing over to a printer,
with some simple instructions or a model for them to follow for style?
No doubt some printers would do an adequate job in these circumstances. General printers often keep sample books of stationery and
other items for customers who are not sure what they really want – or
they can put people in touch with sympathetic designers. Alternatively,
you may be tempted by the advertising which promises that as soon
as you load desktop publishing software into your computer you can
turn out professional quality material.

A point made by the typographer Beatrice Warde, over 30 years ago,
is still valid today. When practically every artefact is offered mass-
produced and ready-made, printing is still made to order. This is
unusual in a world which has elsewhere almost forgotten how to
commission skilled workers to produce specific objects. And, whether
you are designing yourself, or briefing someone else, design sense is
something that you need to acquire.[1]

Beatrice Warde herself believed that design should never impose itself
between the words of the author and the eyes and mind of the reader.
The world has moved on since then and typography in the 1990s seems
often to have left Warde behind. Design does not apologise in the
designer age. It shouts out its presence with large graphic devices,
varieties of type, bold rules, overlaid tints. There is nothing wrong with

this – but anyone producing books or other printed communication should not be tempted to sacrifice the legibility of the words themselves.

This then is the role of the publisher: if printing is made to order, you are the one giving the orders. A knowledge of design becomes necessary, even if you are not planning to do the design work yourself. As a publisher, you are still going to have to make 'design decisions'.

Principles of Design

One of the best ways to learn about design is to look carefully at other people's work. Design is nearly always derivative and there is no copyright on someone else's style. So adapt or imitate anything you think is fit for your purposes.

What you will begin to notice is that design is based on a number of generally accepted aesthetic principles, such as unity, variety, balance, proportion, scale and rhythm.[2] These principles are, of course, as open to challenge in graphic design as they are in any other branch of the visual arts.

If we consider each of these abstract notions in turn it is possible to see how they determine what is a good – or bad – piece of design.

- Unity: All the parts of a design should relate to each other, to provide a homogeneous whole rather than conflicting elements.
- Variety: Within the principle of unity there should be sufficient variety or contrast to maintain interest.
- Balance: This can either be symmetrical or asymmetrical. These terms are defined and discussed below (p.59).
- Proportion: Parts of the design should have an appropriate relationship, for instance in their relative size.
- Scale: The size of any part should bear an appropriate relation to its function.
- Rhythm: There should be harmonious repetition of similar elements.

Many of these principles are best put into practice by using a 'grid', as explained below (pp.64–9).

What to Look For in the Design of a Book
If you look carefully at a piece of printing you should see some of these principles at work. See how the designer has applied these in her or his treatment of the following key points:

- Format.
- Margins.
- Size and style of typefaces used, in both display and text.

- Position and style of illustrations.
- Items of detail, such as captions, chapter openings, quoted material, running heads.
- Cover or jacket design.

Symmetrical and Asymmetrical Design

Typographic designs are usually categorised as either symmetrical (centred) or asymmetrical. It is usual – but not essential – to follow one or other of these styles throughout any particular job. The two styles are explained in diagrammatic form in Figure 5.1 on p.60.

Format

The first decision to be taken when designing a book or any other piece of printed matter is what format it should be. Format is defined as the final page size of the finished book. Although it is technically possible to print and bind a book in virtually any size it is more common, and cheaper, to stick to one of the accepted standard formats. (Formats which are not standard are usually called 'bastard'.)

There are two series of formats commonly in use in the UK. One is the series based on the International Organisation for Standardisation (ISO) standard paper sizes. These are subdivisions of a one square metre sheet, called A0, whose dimensions are 841 x 1189mm. The most familiar division of this is A4, a sheet size of 297 x 210mm, used all over the world for typing, copying and computer paper. This is also a very common size for periodicals.

The other standard series is the British Standard series, of which there are four formats in common use.

There is one size of book which does not fall into either of these series – that used for small paperbacks. There is no British Standard or ISO size for this, and it varies slightly between publishers. The Penguin format is typical, with a trimmed size of 180 x 110mm. This size is sometimes, rather confusingly, called A format. The slightly larger paperback size, often called B format, is in fact the British Standard Large Crown Octavo.

Formats are summarised in Figure 5.2, p.61.

A brief look at the stock of any bookshop which sells a range of campaigning literature would reveal an interesting fact. Commercial publishers very rarely use the ISO series formats for their books whereas small publishers rarely use anything else. Economies of scale are a factor here, since it is slightly cheaper for printers to buy small quantities of paper in ISO sizes. But another reason is the lack of familiarity with the other possibilities. This is strange since the usual paperback sizes ('small paperback' and Large Crown Octavo) make up most of the books on the average reader's shelves. Furthermore, the A5 size, so commonly used by small publishers, is really not a very aesthetic shape for a book,

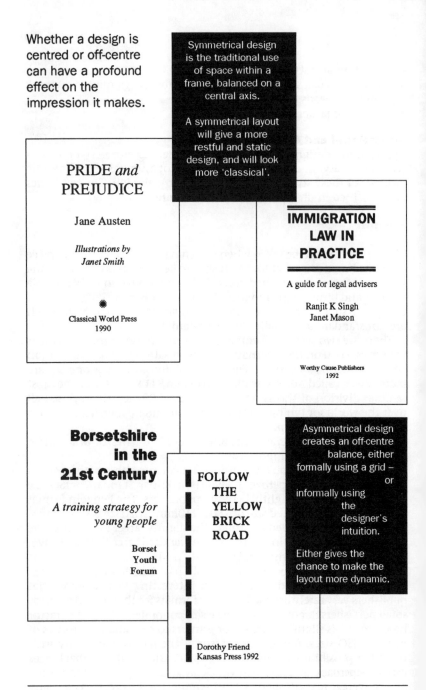

Whether a design is centred or off-centre can have a profound effect on the impression it makes.

Symmetrical design is the traditional use of space within a frame, balanced on a central axis.

A symmetrical layout will give a more restful and static design, and will look more 'classical'.

PRIDE *and*
PREJUDICE

Jane Austen

*Illustrations by
Janet Smith*

✻

Classical World Press
1990

IMMIGRATION
LAW IN
PRACTICE

A guide for legal advisers

Ranjit K Singh
Janet Mason

Worthy Cause Publishers
1992

**Borsetshire
in the
21st Century**

*A training strategy for
young people*

**Borset
Youth
Forum**

FOLLOW
THE
YELLOW
BRICK
ROAD

Dorothy Friend
Kansas Press 1992

Asymmetrical design creates an off-centre balance, either formally using a grid –

or

informally using the designer's intuition.

Either gives the chance to make the layout more dynamic.

Figure 5.1. Symmetrical and asymmetrical design.

with its horizontal:vertical proportions set at a rather squat 1:1.414. Taller and thinner proportions nearer the so-called 'golden section' of the ancient Greeks, which has horizontal:vertical proportions of 1:1.618, have long been preferred by artists, architects and craft workers. It is no coincidence, therefore, that the standard book formats are much closer to these proportions. (See Figure 5.3, p.62.)

ISO series

A0	841	x	1189
A1	594	x	841
A2	420	x	594
A3	297	x	420
A4	210	x	297
A5	148	x	210
A6	105	x	148

British Standard Series (BS 1413: 1970)

	Full size sheet ('quad')	Quarto (1/4 sheet)	Octavo (1/8 sheet)
Crown	768 x 1008	246 x 189	186 x 123
Large Crown	816 x 1056	258 x 201	198 x 129 paperback 'B format'
Demy	888 x 1128	276 x 219	216 x 138
Royal	960 x 1272	312 x 237	234 x 156

Other (not BS series)

Small paperback 'A format'			180 x 110

All figures are for the trimmed size in mm, after approximately 3mm has been trimmed off the head, tail and foredge. To achieve this, the printer uses a bigger size sheet of paper, and trims the book to the exact size after folding.

Figure 5.2. Formats in common use in the UK.

The common use of the A5 size means, however, that it has the advantage of familiarity, or 'user-friendliness'. But its relatively wide format needs a certain amount of careful treatment. Inexperienced publishers sometimes make the mistake of specifying too small a size of type set to too great a measure. This usually makes the type rather illegible. If it is necessary to use most of the width of an A5 page, then it is preferable to keep the type measure relatively short and use the extra space in the margin for something else, such as subheadings, notes or illustrations. (An example of this can be found in the specimen page settings in Figure 5.12, pp.89–93.) Alternatively, a two-column design can be used.

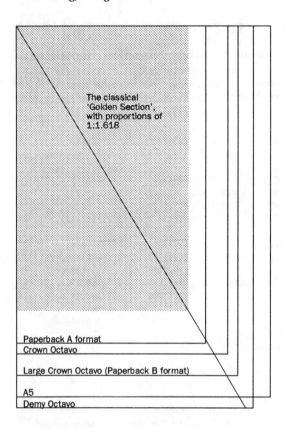

The classical
'Golden Section',
with proportions of
1:1.618

Paperback A format
Crown Octavo

Large Crown Octavo (Paperback B format)

A5
Demy Octavo

Figure 5.3. Various formats, and how their proportions compare.

Larger Format and Landscape Format

There are good reasons for thinking carefully before you decide to produce a larger format book – either the 'quarto' sizes in Figure 5.2, or A4. Bookshops and libraries do not particularly relish bigger sizes, since their shelving and storage do not accommodate them easily. They are even more prejudiced against landscape shape books, where the binding is on the short side of the rectangle. Don't let this stop you from going ahead if you think there are good reasons for producing a larger format book – for instance if you are using illustrations which will look better displayed bigger. But think also of the convenience of your readers. Landscape shape books are difficult to hold while you are reading them, however smart they may look on coffee tables.

Other Factors when Choosing a Format
If you choose any format other than the standard sizes (either ISO or British Standard) then it may be technically possible to print but paper will almost certainly have to be cut away and wasted. So you should discuss this with the printers first. The final 'extent' (length) of your book may be a factor, since even if you can find a paper size which is economical on wastage when you are printing 8 or 16 pages at a time, it may be very wasteful if your extent is not an exact multiple of 8 or 16.

Margins and Grids

Most books or magazines are designed so that each page, or each pair of facing pages (called a 'spread'), is based on a regular repeating pattern. This is called a 'grid' and it provides a structure around which the page is designed. In its simplest form, in a book which contains only text, the grid is nothing more than the space on the page occupied by the typematter. Usually the position of text on the left-hand page is the mirror image of its position on the right-hand page. An illustrated book usually has a more complicated grid to ensure a unified and balanced design.

The word 'grid' is also used to describe the standard preprinted outline cards which many printers will provide for the paste-up of artwork. (See p.115.)

Size of Margins
You will see from Figure 5.4, p.64, that the margins on the outside (foredge) and bottom (tail) are larger than the margins on the inside (back) and top edges. This is the usual practice in 'classical' design. If the margins are exactly equal all round then the eye will see the text as being too low and too far towards the outside edge of the page. What the eye sees as the centre, the 'optical centre', of a page is about 3mm above the true centre. It follows from this, therefore, that if you want to place an item deliberately off centre or low on the page then this must be done by quite a large amount, otherwise it may look like slightly misplaced centring.

How big the margins should be is a matter of both taste and economics. A book with large margins may look more handsome but you will get many fewer words on each page. Mass-market paperbacks can have margins as small as 6mm back, 9mm top and 12mm foredge and tail. In *Methods of Book Design,* Hugh Williamson suggests that a common formula in commercial publishing is 1.5:2:3:4 for back:top:foredge:tail but small publishers might well think that those are rather luxurious. I have found that margins of 10mm back and top and 15mm foredge and tail for Large Crown Octavo and 12mm back and top and 18mm foredge and tail for A5 are adequate but not over-generous. Two recently published Penguins, by comparison, have 13mm back, 15mm top, 10mm foredge and 16mm tail ('small paperback') and 15mm back, 16mm top, 15mm foredge and 20mm tail (Large Crown Octavo).

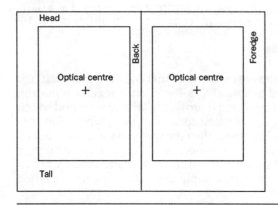

Figure 5.4. 'Classical' proportions for margins, and the optical centre of the type area.

Use of a Grid
A book with illustrations which are to be integrated into the text will probably require a more complicated grid. This should be designed to give maximum flexibility, in order that illustrations and the various items of text get the most suitable arrangement, depending on what impact they are required to make, their subject matter and their relative importance to each other.

A grid is a way of giving a structure to the layout for each page of a book, pamphlet or magazine. It usually comprises a number of vertical columns, subdivided into several horizontal divisions. These are usually mathematically equal, with the result that complete reliance on the grid can lead to very static layouts. The secret is to use a simple grid to give your layout a basic structure – but not to be afraid of breaking it if you want to give imaginative treatment to a particular illustration.

In Figure 5.5 on pp.65–9 some simple one, two and three column grids are shown and discussed.

Dividing the type area into two columns adds further design possibilities. Major headings can be set across the full width, subheadings across one column only.

When the horizontal space is divided into two halves, this increases the possibilities still further, particularly if illustrations are to be used.

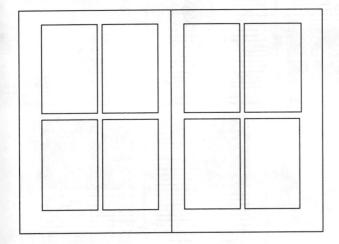

Figure 5.5. Multi-column grids with examples of their use.

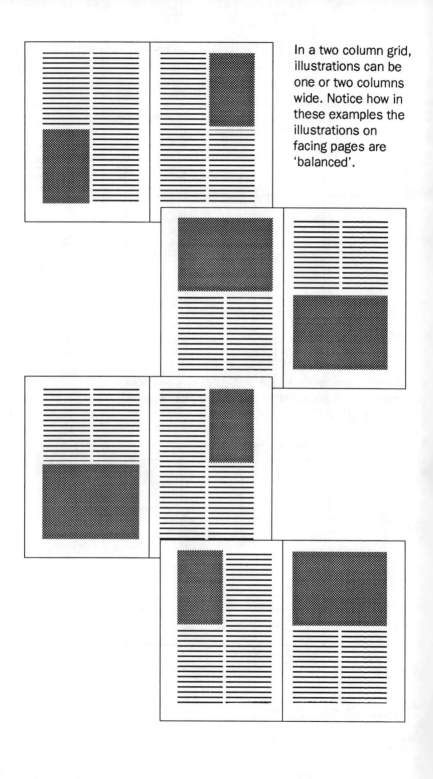

In a two column grid, illustrations can be one or two columns wide. Notice how in these examples the illustrations on facing pages are 'balanced'.

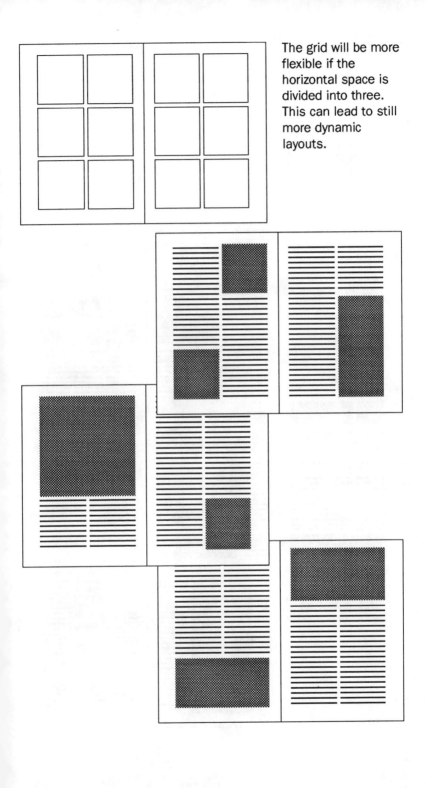

The grid will be more flexible if the horizontal space is divided into three. This can lead to still more dynamic layouts.

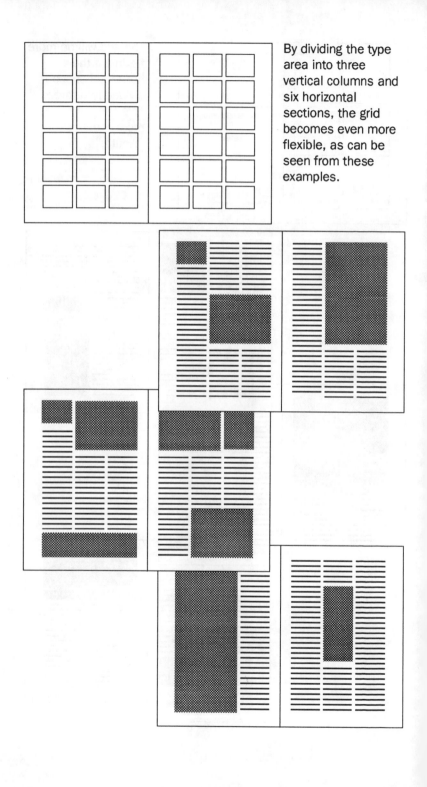

By dividing the type area into three vertical columns and six horizontal sections, the grid becomes even more flexible, as can be seen from these examples.

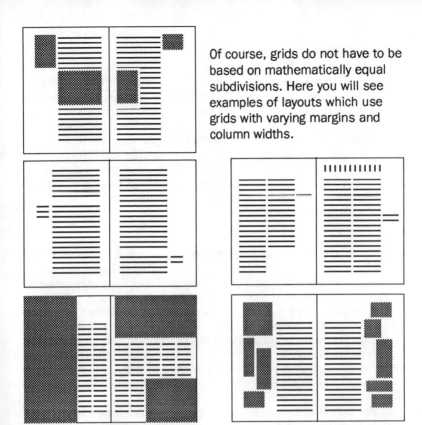

Of course, grids do not have to be based on mathematically equal subdivisions. Here you will see examples of layouts which use grids with varying margins and column widths.

Type and Typefaces

The range of typefaces now offered by many typesetters and DTP programs can be bewilderingly large. This is because the cost of the addition of new faces to the systems now in common use is quite small compared with the cost of the system itself.

Aesthetic reasons often govern the choice of one typeface over another. They may be difficult to explain, since a particular design may just 'feel' right. The best way of developing this 'feel' for typefaces is by studying them. You can start quite simply, by looking critically at books (you sometimes find the typeface listed on the title-page verso). Some specimens are also shown in this book, Figure 5.8, pp.75–8.

Although recent years have seen a revolution in the way in which type is set and printed the essential element has not changed since Gutenberg and the invention of printing in the Western world around 1440. Gutenberg devised a method whereby a piece of text was assembled (or 'set') from the individual letters (pieces of 'type') and took impressions on sheets of paper from this. These basic systems of metal typesetting and letterpress printing still survive today and are outlined in Chapters 6 and 8 (pp.99 and 131).

However, most printing is now done by offset lithography (see pp.131–2) and most typesetting employs an imagesetting method, where individual letterforms are assembled from computerised images rather than pieces of metal. Some feel that there has been a reduction in standards and quality as the industry moved from one technology to another. But the expansion of DTP, imagesetting and litho printing has led to greater freedom and flexibility for the designer, a significant improvement in working conditions and, perhaps most importantly for the small publisher, the greater availability and cheapness of printing for the ordinary person.

Type Classification

Gutenberg and his immediate successors printed in what typographers call 'Black Letter', the correct name for what is sometimes called Gothic or Old English type. This was because they were concerned to produce their books in the same style as the scribes of the day. Printing spread rapidly across Europe, with William Caxton printing the first book in English in Belgium in 1475 and setting up the first press in England a year later. Within 25 years of the invention of printing, black letter type was already being superseded by what is now called the Roman letter, as the centre of great printing moved to Italy. It is still argued by some that the finest and most readable typefaces ever designed were the first types of this era.

In the development of 'seriffed' type, where the letters have small terminal strokes at an angle to the main strokes, a number of changes have occurred since. There is not space to go into the details of type classification, although a summary of the standard system is shown in Figure 5.7, opposite. From this you can see that there are four basic classes of seriffed type – Old Face, Transitional, Modern and Slab Serif. It is useful to know a little about type classification if for no other reason than one useful design maxim is that seriffed type from different classes should not be mixed. (Like all such maxims, this can be broken if you so wish!)

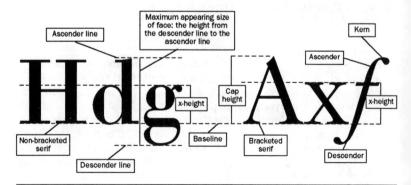

Figure 5.6. Terms used in describing the design of a typeface.

Old face (Humanist/Garalde) Aeg	Designs based on the earliest roman types from the 14th century, with oblique strokes and without pronounced contrast between thick and thin strokes. Examples include Centaur, Caslon, Bembo (here), Garamond.
Transitional Aeg	Later designs, which still have oblique stress and bracketed serifs but also have more pronounced contrast between thick and thin strokes. Examples include Baskerville, Bell and Plantin (here).
Modern (Didone) Aeg	Abrupt contrast between thick and thin strokes, horizontal and vertical stress, often unbracketed serifs. Examples include Bodoni (here), Caledonia, Melior.
Slab serif Aeg	Heavy square-ended serifs, with or without brackets. Examples include Beton, Clarendon, Rockwell (here).
Sans serif (Lineale) Aeg	No serifs. Varying contrast between thick and thin strokes, depending on whether they are Grotesque (e.g Franklin Gothic, as here, or Helvetica), Geometric (e.g. Futura, Folio) or Humanist (e.g. Gill Sans, Optima).
Decorative (Graphic/Glyphic) Aeg	Designs based on drawn, chiselled or calligraphic forms. Examples of Graphic faces include Uncial, Klang. Examples of Glyphic faces include Albertus, Castellar, Flare Serif (here).
Script *Aeg*	*Typefaces that imitate script or handwriting, either formally, (e.g. Palace Script) or informally, (e.g. Brush Script, as here, or Mistral).*

Figure 5.7. Classification of typefaces.

The first 'sans serif' (non-seriffed) typefaces appeared in printing in the early nineteenth century, although they had been used by stone-masons and signwriters long before they were first used by printers. At the beginning of the twentieth century they became very popular. Their biggest single boost was probably the commission from the London Underground to Edward Johnston, the lettering artist, for the design for a typeface. His design is still used by London Regional Transport in a modified version. It was also adapted later by his pupil Eric Gill for the famous Gill Sans typeface.

The Terminology of Type

The section above has already introduced a number of terms commonly used by people who work with type. Before we go any further it will be useful to define some further terms.

Collective terms for type are, first of all, the 'fount' or 'font', which is the collection of individual forms of one size and one design, covering the alphabet, figures, punctuation and special sorts. Secondly, there is the 'series', which is a number of founts of different sizes of an identical design. Thus we get the Times Roman series. Thirdly, there is the 'family', which is a group of series from a single basic design each with a variation in weight, width, italicisation or some special feature. The Times family therefore consists of many different series: Roman, Italic, Bold, Bold Italic and special features such as Extended, Light, Semibold and so on.

What an individual typeface looks like on the page is governed by a number of factors in its design. Some of these are defined in Figure 5.6, p.70. From the point of view of the publisher and aside from any aesthetic considerations, the most important factors are the 'set' and the 'x-height'. Set is defined as the width of each individual character and is therefore important for determining how many characters will fit into a given space. The average set is used to prepare copyfitting tables (see Figure 5.11, p.84). The x-height is what it sounds like, the height of the lower case x (and hence of other lower case characters such as a, c, e, etc.). The greater the x-height in relation to the extending portion in b, d, f, etc. ('ascenders') and in g, j, p, etc. ('descenders'), the larger the type will appear to be. It is therefore possible that the 10pt size of a face with a larger x-height and set will look as big as the 11pt size of a face with a smaller x-height and set.

Thus this could be important when choosing a typeface, particularly if you want to fit a lot of text into a small number of pages or, conversely, to 'bump out' a small amount of text into a thicker book. These factors are discussed below, in the section on choosing a typeface, pp.74–9.

The Point System and the Pica Em
Although the printing industry in the UK has been almost completely metricated, typesizes have not. In the UK (and also the USA) the size of type is measured in points, and one point is defined as 0.13837 inches. This means that there are approximately 72pts to the inch. (In the rest of Europe, type is measured in a similar unit called the Didot point: the Didot point is slightly bigger than the UK/US point.)

The point system is also used to measure the distance between lines of type. This 'interlinear space' is usually still referred to by its old name, 'leading', a word that derives from the days of handsetting metal type when space was created by inserting thin lead strips between the lines of type.

The legibility of many typefaces is improved if they are set with extra interlinear space, usually one or two points. Modern typesetting systems can be instructed to do this automatically. Type that is to be set with interlinear space is usually referred to as, for example, 10pt on an 11pt 'body', and written 10/11pt. Desktop publishing programs often put 'automatic' leading between lines. This is usually preset at about 20 per cent of the body size.

In the days of metal typesetting, typesizes usually started at 6pt (a very small size usually used only for newspaper classified advertisements). They then rose in single point steps up to 14pt. This was followed by an 18pt size, and then sizes increased by 6pt steps until 48pt. The steps generally went up by 12pt or more, usually to a maximum of 72pt. You are unlikely to need anything bigger than 72pt for book or pamphlet publishing, although in newspapers the sizes go much higher still. Modern imagesetters and professional quality DTP programs can usually set type in any size between 6pt and 128pt – sometimes bigger still – and are not confined to these sizes. For the sake of convenience, however, most typesetters show their range just in these divisions.

While typesize is expressed in points, the 'measure', or width to which the type is set, is expressed differently. It is always described by its width in 12pt ems, often called pica ems or picas (pronounced 'pie-kah'). This term will require some explanation. An 'em' is the unit of measurement which is the square of any given body height. It is the usual space for indentation at the beginning of a new paragraph. Thus when setting 8pt type, the indent is a square space, an em of 8pts by 8pts; when setting 14pt type, the indent is an em 14pts by 14pts. However, it is immaterial what the size of the type is when specifying its measure or width. Measure is always specified in 12pt ems even if the typesize is other than 12pt. Throughout this book measure is always specified in pica ems.

The words em and en derive from being approximately the spaces occupied by the capital letters M and N.

A number of books about the terminology of type are listed in the Further Reading section, pp.150–3.

Choosing a Text Typeface

Before choosing the particular typeface for your job you should examine lists of typefaces provided by your typesetters and, if possible, a specimen piece of setting provided by the system's manufacturer. There are major differences in some typefaces between one manufacturer and another, both in design and size, so it is important to look at precisely what you will be using. If it is impossible to get hold of manufacturer's specimens, then at least ask for other pieces of printing from setting provided by your typesetter. This advice is even more appropriate if you are doing your own typesetting using DTP, where typefaces vary widely in quality from one system to another.

A number of specimens are shown in this book, in Figure 5.8, pp.75–8.

There are a number of factors to consider when choosing a typeface. The following are adapted from criteria proposed by the typographer Oliver Simon. [3]

1. Width and height of letters.
2. Contrast between thick and thin strokes.
3. Size of capitals.
4. General weight and colour.

These differences, as we will see, are of practical importance, besides affecting the look of the typeface.

Width and Height of Letters These factors have been discussed briefly above (p.72) when the definitions of x-height and set were explained. The two combined give the overall size of the type on its body. By comparing the specimens in Figure 5.8 (pp.75–8) you can see that although they are all set in 11pt, the length of the alphabet varies in both capitals and lower case. This affects the number of words that can be set in a line and hence on a page. In addition, if a face has a large x-height, such as Times or Baskerville, it will look a lot better if it is 'leaded', that is set with a space (usually one or two points) between each line. This is because a large x-height means that the ascenders and descenders are quite short. The typeface looks very cramped if it is set without extra space between the lines.

However, if you look again at Times and compare it with Bembo, which has a much smaller x-height, you will see that their set is much the same. The combination of these factors, being large on the body and narrow of set, is what makes Times such a useful all-round typeface.

ABCDEFGHIJKLMNOPQRSTUVWXYZ
abcdefghijklmnopqrstuvwxyz

The sight of this far from typical demonstration aroused considerable interest because of the predominance of women. A woman from the **Post Office Engineers in Enfield** held up a placard: 'We want the chance to prove we can do the work of any man.' 'All my own work,' she commented as I scribbled it down. *Pottery workers from Stoke-on-Trent carried 'Equal Pay Now' and 'We make mugs but we are not mugs!'*

11/12pt Bembo

ABCDEFGHIJKLMNOPQRSTUVWXYZ
abcdefghijklmnopqrstuvwxyz

The sight of this far from typical demonstration aroused considerable interest because of the predominance of women. A woman from the **Post Office Engineers in Enfield** held up a placard: 'We want the chance to prove we can do the work of any man.' 'All my own work,' she commented as I scribbled it down. *Pottery workers from Stoke-on-Trent carried 'Equal Pay Now' and 'We make mugs but we are not mugs!'*

11/12pt Bodoni

ABCDEFGHIJKLMNOPQRSTUVWXYZ
abcdefghijklmnopqrstuvwxyz

The sight of this far from typical demonstration aroused considerable interest because of the predominance of women. A woman from the **Post Office Engineers in Enfield** held up a placard: 'We want a chance to prove we can do the work of any man.' 'All my own work,' she commented as I scribbled it down. *Pottery workers from Stoke on Trent carried 'Equal Pay Now' and 'We make mugs but we are not mugs!'*

Figure 5.8. Examples of various typefaces suitable for text setting. Although all are set in 11/12pt, there are, as can be seen, considerable variations in appearing size, 'set' (which defines the breadth of individual letterforms) and the necessity for leading to improve legibility.

11/12pt Century Old Style

ABCDEFGHIJKLMNOPQRSTUVWXYZ
abcdefghijklmnopqrstuvwxyz

The sight of this far from typical demonstration aroused
considerable interest because of the predominance of women. A
woman from the **Post Office Engineers in Enfield** held up a
placard: 'We want a chance to prove we can do the work of any
man'. 'All my own work', she commented as I scribbled it down.
Pottery workers from Stoke on Trent carried 'Equal Pay Now' and
'We make mugs but we are not mugs!'

11/12pt Ehrhardt

ABCDEFGHIJKLMNOPQRSTUVWXYZ
abcdefghijklmnopqrstuvwxyz

The sight of this far from typical demonstration aroused considerable
interest because of the predominance of women. A woman from the **Post
Office Engineers in Enfield** held up a placard: 'We want a chance to
prove we can do the work of any man.' 'All my own work,' she commented
as I scribbled it down. *Pottery workers from Stoke on Trent carried 'Equal Pay*
Now' and 'We make mugs but we are not mugs!'

11/12pt Garamond

ABCDEFGHIJKLMNOPQRSTUVWXYZ
abcdefghijklmnopqrstuvwxyz

The sight of this far from typical demonstration aroused considerable
interest because of the predominance of women. A woman from the
Post Office Engineers in Enfield held up a placard: 'We want the
chance to prove we can do the work of any man.' 'All my own work,' she
commented as I scribbled it down. *Pottery workers from Stoke-on-Trent*
carried 'Equal Pay Now' and 'We make mugs but we are not mugs!'

11/12pt Joanna

ABCDEFGHIJKLMNOPQRSTUVWXYZ
abcdefghijklmnopqrstuvwxyz

The sight of this far from typical demonstration aroused considerable
interest because of the predominance of women. A woman from the **Post
Office Engineers in Enfield** held up a placard: 'We want the chance to
prove we can do the work of any man.' 'All my own work,' she
commented as I scribbled it down. Pottery workers from Stoke-on-Trent carried
'Equal Pay Now' and 'We make mugs but we are not mugs!'

ABCDEFGHIJKLMNOPQRSTUVWXYZ
abcdefghijklmnopqrstuvwxyz

The sight of this far from typical demonstration aroused considerable interest because of the predominance of women. A woman from the **Post Office Engineers in Enfield** held up a placard: 'We want a chance to prove we can do the work of any man'. 'All my own work', she commented as I scribbled it down. *Pottery workers from Stoke on Trent carried 'Equal Pay Now' and 'We make mugs but we are not mugs!'*

ABCDEFGHIJKLMNOPQRSTUVWXYZ
abcdefghijklmnopqrstuvwxyz

The sight of this far from typical demonstration aroused considerable interest because of the predominance of women. A woman from the **Post Office Engineers in Enfield** held up a placard: 'We want a chance to prove we can do the work of any man'. 'All my own work', she commented as I scribbled it down. *Pottery workers from Stoke on Trent carried 'Equal Pay Now' and 'We make mugs but we are not mugs!'*

ABCDEFGHIJKLMNOPQRSTUVWXYZ
abcdefghijklmnopqrstuvwxyz

The sight of this far from typical demonstration aroused considerable interest because of the predominance of women. A woman from the **Post Office Engineers in Enfield** held up a placard: 'We want the chance to prove we can do the work of any man.' 'All my own work,' she commented as I scribbled it down. *Pottery workers from Stoke-on-Trent carried 'Equal Pay Now' and 'We make mugs but we are not mugs!'*

ABCDEFGHIJKLMNOPQRSTUVWXYZ
abcdefghijklmnopqrstuvwxyz

The sight of this far from typical demonstration aroused considerable interest because of the predominance of women. A woman from the **Post Office Engineers in Enfield** held up a placard: 'We want a chance to prove we can do the work of any man'. 'All my own work', she commented as I scribbled it down. *Pottery workers from Stoke on Trent carried 'Equal Pay Now' and 'We make mugs but we are not mugs!'*

ABCDEFGHIJKLMNOPQRSTUVWXYZ
abcdefghijklmnopqrstuvwxyz

The sight of this far from typical demonstration aroused considerable interest because of the predominance of women. A woman from the **Post Office Engineers in Enfield** held up a placard: 'We want a chance to prove we can do the work of any man'. 'All my own work', she commented as I scribbled it down. *Pottery workers from Stoke on Trent carried 'Equal Pay Now' and 'We make mugs but we are not mugs!'*

ABCDEFGHIJKLMNOPQRSTUVWXYZ
abcdefghijklmnopqrstuvwxyz

The sight of this far from typical demonstration aroused considerable interest because of the predominance of women. A woman from the **Post Office Engineers in Enfield** held up a placard: 'We want a chance to prove we can do the work of any man'. 'All my own work', she commented as I scribbled it down. *Pottery workers from Stoke on Trent carried 'Equal Pay Now' and 'We make mugs but we are not mugs!'*

ABCDEFGHIJKLMNOPQRSTUVWXYZ
abcdefghijklmnopqrstuvwxyz

The sight of this far from typical demonstration aroused considerable interest because of the predominance of women. A woman from the **Post Office Engineers in Enfield** held up a placard: 'We want the chance to prove we can do the work of any man.' 'All my own work,' she commented as I scribbled it down. *Pottery workers from Stoke-on-Trent carried 'Equal Pay Now' and 'We make mugs but we are not mugs!'*

ABCDEFGHIJKLMNOPQRSTUVWXYZ
abcdefghijklmnopqrstuvwxyz

The sight of this far from typical demonstration aroused considerable interest because of the predominance of women. A woman from the **Post Office Engineers in Enfield** held up a placard: 'We want a chance to prove we can do the work of any man'. 'All my own work', she commented as I scribbled it down. *Pottery workers from Stoke on Trent carried 'Equal Pay Now' and 'We make mugs but we are not mugs!'*

Contrast Between Thick and Thin Strokes Typefaces which have major contrast between thick and thin strokes are those from the Transitional and Modern classes (see Figure 5.7, p.71). In the specimens, Times and Plantin are examples of Transitional faces and Bodoni is a Modern face. These nearly all benefit from being set with leading, to avoid the dazzling effect they appear to produce when set solid.

Size of Capitals The capitals of most typefaces are the height of the ascenders but in a few, such as Bembo and Palatino, they are a little lower. This can be useful if your book has a lot of capitalisation in the text or is, say, a bibliography or a catalogue.

General Weight and Colour Some typefaces are much darker and heavier than others. These include Plantin, Times and Ehrhardt, while others such as Bembo and Garamond appear very light in both colour and weight. In general, heavier types will be more legible if you are going to be printing on a shiny 'coated' paper. (For types of paper, see p.135.) Leading, or its absence, also affects the apparent darkness.

Legibility Legibility is a further factor to take into account when choosing a typeface. This is slightly different from the considerations above in that it is not just an inherent quality in a typeface's design but is affected by how it is treated. Ruari McLean in *Typography* sets out three rules:[4]

1. Sans serif type is intrinsically less legible than seriffed type.
2. A well-designed roman upper and lower case piece of setting is easier to read than any variant, such as capitals, italic, bold, expanded or condensed.
3. Words should be set close together (with average space between them no greater than that taken by the letter 'i') and there should be more space between lines than between words.

The use for text of sans serif type like Gill, Helvetica or Univers, or slab serif type, like Rockwell or Stymie, is not recommended for a book with continuous text, because sans serif and slab serif are intrinsically less legible. If in any doubt, use a well-designed seriffed typeface. The specimens in Figure 5.8, pp.75–8, should help you assess some typefaces for their legibility.

Justification
Type that is set with even right- and left-hand margins is called 'justified'. Type set to a left-hand margin only is called 'ranged left' and to a right-hand margin, 'ranged right'. In justified setting, the typesetting program calculates how much space to leave between each word

when the line end is reached. Justified type set to narrow measures often results in large spaces between words, which may look unsightly and also affect legibility. Hyphenation of longer words can reduce the frequency of large wordspaces, but can result in more problems if it is carried out automatically (see p.103).

Some legibility studies have indicated that ranged left type is, in fact, easier to read than justified. Be that as it may, the vast majority of books are still set justified.

Ranged right typesetting is difficult to read in continuous text and its use should generally be confined to display setting and captions, etc.

If you are using a typewriter, or an IBM Composer, for typesetting, then ranged left typesetting will be cheaper and simpler.

Choosing a Display Typeface

A 'display' typeface is one which is used for headings for chapters or parts and the title page and cover. It is possible to use a large size of the text typeface, or perhaps a variant such as its related bold or italic. Alternatively, you might prefer to choose a different face altogether. This can be chosen either to complement the text or to provide a contrast.

A huge number of faces exist – many more than are used for text typesetting – and many of these may be suitable. A quick look through a typical big range, such as the Letraset catalogues, will show you that many display faces are extremely quirky. So if you are not sure whether something will work or not, then you are probably better off not using it.

There are two simple rules which will help you choose a 'safe' display face. The first is, do not mix seriffed type from different type classes. (Type classification is set out in Figure 5.7, p.71.) Therefore do not use a Modern display face like Bodoni, with major contrast between thick and thin strokes, with an Old Style text face like Garamond, which has more graduated contrast.

The second rule is, have regard to the overall 'colour' of the page you will be creating. If you have long chapter titles then a very dark, rather expanded typeface such as Gill Extra Bold or Plantin Bold set in a large size will be too over-powering. On the other hand, a thin condensed face such as Joanna will be too weak if there is only a small amount of display.

Some useful display typefaces readily available are shown in Figure 5.9, opposite, together with some text typefaces they complement. See also the section below, pp.86–7, on the mark-up of title page and chapter headings.

Gill Sans Extra Bold

can be used as a display typeface. Here it is contrasted with text set in Bembo. Gill's clean lines and strength make it possible to combine it with many other text faces.

Bodoni Medium is too light

when combined with a serif face from a different type classification like Caslon as here. It is better to provide contrast by using a much heavier weight, such as

Bodoni Bold Italic

which provides both colour and variety. Here it is combined with text set in Plantin. Although Plantin is a transitional face and Bodoni a modern, their darkness means they can complement each other.

News Gothic is a thin and

rather condensed sans serif face. It looks best when combined with another thin face, such as Perpetua. This is shown in this example. The whole effect will be to make the page very light.

Rockwell Bold being

a slab serif combines well with a number of seriffed fonts. It can also be used to provide contrast to a light sans serif, like Franklin Gothic, if some text is to be set in this.

FUTURA EXTRA BOLD CONDENSED

is a very dark, very condensed display typeface, which is excellent for long headings since it does not take up too much space. It combines well with most seriffed faces. Here it is shown with Palatino.

Joanna Italic and other light

italics, and other rather exotic faces, like scripts, can also be used if you want to make a *real* contrast and there is not *too* much display setting. Here it is set with the body text in Gill Bold. You might not want to read a whole book in this, however!

Figure 5.9. Various display typefaces, and some text typefaces they complement.

Mark-up

Having chosen the typefaces for both text and display you are now in a position to begin the detailed 'mark-up' of the typescript. In many ways this is a parallel operation to the copy-editing process described in Chapter 3. It involves giving the typesetter clear and unambiguous instructions for each piece of matter which is to appear in print. If you are responsible both for editing and designing your publication (a not uncommon situation for the small publisher) then you may be able to do some of this work, such as coding subheads as explained on p.41, while you are doing the detailed copy-edit. Or you may find it easier to concentrate just on copy-editing while you are reading the typescript thoroughly and then go back through it again (without reading it!) for the mark-up phase.

The laborious process of marking every single piece of copy with correct instructions for the typesetter is not necessary. You can provide typesetters with an instruction sheet listing all the items that they will want to know. An example is shown in Figure 5.10, opposite. (This is similar to setting up 'styles' in a DTP program.) The purpose of the next section of this chapter is to show you both how to fill in this instruction sheet accurately and how to achieve in practice the creative design you have devised.

The Text Page

We have already discussed format, margins and grids (pp.59–69). What you have to do now is to design the text within these parameters. The place to begin is with the ordinary text page, since this is the book's basic unit.

In its simplest form, the text page may consist of nothing more than text and a page number (usually called a 'folio'). But it may have other elements which are considered below.

The most vital decision is the size of type and the width or 'measure' to which it is to be set. You are aiming for a balance which will give you not too many – and not too few – characters in the line for easy reading. You also have to bear in mind the overall costs of your book. There is no hard and fast rule as to how wide you should set any particular size of any particular typeface but a good rule of thumb for a book for normal reading is to aim for an average number of between 60 and 70 characters per line. You can calculate what sizes and measures give you this average from the copyfitting table shown in Figure 5.11, p.84. To give you some idea of what are optimum sizes, Times Roman set on the Linotron system has an average of 53 characters in a 20 pica em line when set in 10pt, and 61 characters in a 26 pica em line when set in 12pt.

Small Publishing Co-op
456 Worthy Road
London N29 9KL

Typesetting/DTP Instructions

Title Council Tenants Rights **Author** Jones

Series Rights Guide

Typesetter/DTP ACE DTP

Layouts herewith Series style

Copy/disks herewith Text/prelims + Disk: WordPerfect 5.1 (PC)

Copy/disks to follow index

Margins (after trimming) Head 20mm Back 20mm Foredge 30mm Tail 30mm

Main text 11/12pt Plantin x 20 ems (2 cols) **Paragraph indent** 1 em

Chapter titles 36pt Gill Extra Bold x 44 ems

Drop None _____ Space after 6 lines

Chapters Start new page/run on

Subheads A 13pt Plantin Bold Space above 15pt below 6pt

B _____ — Space above ____ below ____

C _____ — Space above ____ below ____

Quoted matter As text _____ Full out/indented 1 em

Illustrations 6 cartoons (attached)

Captions None

Headlines Left 8pt CAPS centred Folio } 11/12pt fig
Right 8pt CAPS centred Folio } at foot

Footnotes/endnotes 9/11pt at end chapter

Footnote references Superior figures/symbols

Prelims ½ title; blank; title; verso; contents; blank = 6pp in all

Prelims numbered in/roman numbers

List of references/bibliography None

Index Author will supply

Other end matter None

Proofs required straight to page, with illus. in posn.

Signed J. Jones **Date** 1/12/92

Figure 5.10. Publisher's instruction sheet for typesetters.

Length of lower case alphabet (in pts)	Number of characters per pica em	Measure of line to be set (in pica ems)																					
		7	8	9	10	11	12	13	14	15	16	17	18	19	20	22	24	26	28	30	32	34	36
60	5.80	41	46	52	58	64	70	75	81	87	93	99	104	110	116	128	139	151	162	174	186	197	209
62	5.61	39	45	51	56	62	67	73	79	84	90	95	101	107	112	123	135	146	157	168	180	191	202
64	5.44	38	44	49	54	60	65	71	76	82	87	92	98	103	109	120	131	141	152	163	174	185	196
66	5.27	37	42	47	53	58	63	69	74	79	84	90	95	100	105	116	126	137	148	158	169	179	190
68	5.12	36	41	46	51	56	61	67	72	77	82	87	92	97	102	113	123	133	143	154	164	174	184
70	4.97	35	40	45	50	55	60	65	70	75	80	84	89	94	99	109	119	129	139	149	159	169	179
72	4.83	34	39	43	48	53	58	63	68	72	77	82	87	92	96	106	116	126	135	145	155	164	174
74	4.70	33	38	42	47	52	56	61	66	70	75	80	85	89	94	103	113	122	132	141	150	160	169
76	4.58	32	37	41	46	50	55	60	64	69	73	78	82	87	92	101	110	119	128	137	147	156	165
78	4.46	31	36	40	45	49	54	58	62	67	71	76	80	85	89	98	107	116	125	134	143	152	161
80	4.35	30	35	39	44	48	52	57	61	65	70	74	78	83	87	96	104	113	122	131	139	148	157
82	4.24	30	34	38	42	47	51	55	59	64	68	72	76	81	85	93	102	110	119	127	136	144	153
84	4.14	29	33	37	41	46	50	54	58	62	66	70	75	79	83	91	99	108	116	124	133	141	149
86	4.05	28	32	36	40	45	49	53	57	61	65	69	73	77	81	89	97	105	113	121	129	138	146
88	3.95	28	32	36	40	43	47	51	55	59	63	67	71	75	79	87	95	103	111	119	127	134	142
90	3.87	27	31	35	39	43	46	50	54	58	62	66	70	73	77	85	93	101	108	116	124	131	139
92	3.78	26	30	34	38	42	45	49	53	57	61	64	68	72	76	83	91	98	106	113	121	129	136
94	3.70	26	30	33	37	41	44	48	52	56	59	63	67	70	74	81	89	96	104	111	118	126	133
96	3.63	25	29	33	36	40	44	47	51	54	58	62	65	69	73	80	87	94	102	109	116	123	131
98	3.55	25	28	32	36	39	43	46	50	53	57	60	64	67	71	78	85	92	99	107	114	121	128
100	3.48	24	28	31	35	38	42	45	49	52	56	59	63	66	70	77	84	90	97	104	111	118	125
102	3.41	24	27	31	34	38	41	44	48	51	55	58	61	65	68	75	82	89	96	102	109	116	123
104	3.35	23	27	30	33	37	40	43	47	50	54	57	60	64	67	74	80	87	94	100	107	114	120
106	3.28	23	26	30	33	36	39	42	45	49	53	56	59	62	66	72	79	85	92	98	105	112	118
108	3.22	23	26	29	32	35	39	42	45	48	52	55	58	61	64	71	77	84	90	97	103	110	116
110	3.16	22	25	28	32	35	38	41	44	47	51	54	57	60	63	70	76	82	89	95	101	108	114
112	3.11	22	25	28	31	34	37	40	43	47	50	53	56	59	62	68	75	81	87	93	99	106	112
114	3.05	21	24	27	31	34	37	40	43	46	49	52	55	58	61	67	73	79	85	92	98	104	110
116	3.00	21	24	27	30	33	36	39	42	45	48	51	54	57	60	66	72	78	84	90	96	102	108
118	2.95	21	24	27	29	32	35	38	41	44	47	50	53	56	59	65	71	77	83	88	94	100	106
120	2.90	20	23	26	29	32	35	38	41	44	46	49	52	55	58	64	70	75	81	87	93	99	104
122	2.85	20	23	26	29	31	34	37	40	43	46	48	51	54	57	63	68	74	80	86	91	97	103
124	2.81	20	22	25	28	31	34	36	39	42	45	48	50	53	56	62	67	73	79	84	90	95	101
126	2.76	19	22	25	28	30	33	36	39	41	44	47	50	52	55	61	66	72	77	83	88	94	99
128	2.72	19	22	24	27	30	33	35	38	41	44	46	49	52	54	60	65	71	76	82	87	92	98
130	2.68	19	21	24	27	29	32	35	37	40	43	46	48	51	54	59	64	70	75	80	86	91	96
135	2.58	18	21	23	26	28	31	34	36	39	41	44	46	49	52	57	62	67	72	78	83	88	93
140	2.49	17	20	22	25	27	30	32	35	37	40	42	45	47	50	55	60	65	70	75	80	85	89
145	2.40	17	19	22	24	26	29	31	34	36	38	41	43	46	48	53	58	62	67	72	77	82	86
150	2.32	16	19	21	23	26	28	30	32	35	37	39	42	44	46	51	56	60	65	70	74	79	84
155	2.25	16	18	20	22	25	27	29	31	34	36	38	40	42	45	49	54	58	63	67	72	76	81
160	2.18	15	17	20	22	24	26	28	30	33	35	37	39	41	44	48	52	57	61	65	70	74	78
165	2.11	15	17	19	21	23	25	27	30	32	34	36	38	40	42	46	51	55	59	63	67	72	76
170	2.05	14	16	18	20	23	25	27	29	31	33	35	37	38	40	44	48	52	56	60	64	70	74
175	1.99	14	16	18	20	22	24	26	29	30	32	34	36	38	40	44	48	52	56	60	64	68	72

This table can be used to calculate the number of lines a given piece of copy will fill when set in any typeface, at any size and measure, if the length of the lowercase alphabet in that size is known, and it has been set on the same system using the same unit spacing.

abcdefghijklmnopqrstuvwxyz   12pt Monotype Plantin
◀—————— 155pts ——————▶

Measure the alphabet length in points, and select the number nearest to the alphabet length from the first column. The corresponding number in the second column is the number of characters per pica em, and the number of characters in the measure can be calculated simply by multiplying this figure by the measure in pica ems. Therefore in this example, an alphabet length of 155pts gives a reading of 2.25 characters per pica em. If set to a measure of 24 pica ems there will be an average of 54 characters per line.

Figure 5.11. Copyfitting table.

Headlines (Running Heads) A book is often improved by having headlines (sometimes called running heads) at the top of each page. Traditionally these consist of the title of the book on the left-hand page and the title of the chapter on the right. It is possible to combine the headline with the folio – useful if you are short of space and do not want to waste a line of type on a headline alone. The headline is often set in italic or small capitals in the same size as the text type. It should not intrude too much on the rest of the page. A fine rule or some such other device can also be used.

Subheadings Many non-fiction books have chapters which are broken into sections with subheadings. A complicated book will often have more than one 'grade' of subheading to denote both sections and subsections. Where this occurs it is usual to distinguish these by 'colour'. Thus the major subheading may be set in bold type, while the minor one is set in italic, as bold is darker than italic.

At least one line should be left blank (sometimes called a 'line space' or a 'white line') between the last line of previous text and the subheading. The page will probably look better for having two or more white lines.

Although the subheading may be set in a slightly bigger size type than the text it should not be too large. If its typesize is larger than that used for the text, then the space before and after the subheading should be adjusted so that heading and space together take up the equivalent space of an exact number of lines of text.

Coding of subheadings is explained on p.41.

Footnotes Where these occur, they are usually set in type at least two points smaller than the text size and separated from the text by a line space. Large numbers of notes are better dealt with in a number sequence and set either at the end of the chapter or the end of the book. (See references, pp.44–50.)

Quoted Matter Quotations of more than about five lines are usually set apart from the rest of the text in separate paragraphs (see p.40). They are distinguished from the text on the printed page often just by indenting the matter from the left-hand margin only, or from both margins, or by setting the matter in italic or a smaller size of text type.

Preliminary Matter

Half-title Page The half-title is not regarded as a page for special display: it may be only the title of the book or it may also contain a blurb, extracts from reviews or the author's biography. These are usually all set in smaller type than the text.

Title Page The title page should foreshadow what comes in the rest of the book and be an integral part of the overall design. Many designers leave its detailed design to a late stage in production since this allows more time for ideas to germinate. Where a book is printed in more than one section, the first section is usually the last to be printed, since printers are well aware that publishers often make last-minute alterations to the preliminary matter.

The copy which should appear on the title page has already been discussed (see p.27). The designer has to decide how this can be composed in a title page which is informative, interesting and in keeping with the rest of the book. It must also harmonise with any frontispiece illustration appearing on the left-hand page facing it.

If you are publishing just a short book or pamphlet then you may have decided to dispense with a half-title. In this case the title page will be the first inside page of your publication and there cannot be a frontispiece.

Because there is comparatively little to say on the title page the correct balance of type and space is important. A frequent method used to link the title page to the rest of the text is to define the equivalent of the type area on the title page by rules or a border.

Particular attention should also be paid to the line breaks in the display type, in both symmetrical and asymmetrical layouts. Try to avoid awkward shapes, such as those with all the weight at the top or bottom. For example:

>   Highways and
>   Byways of the
>   Yorkshire
>   Dales

is better than:

>   Highways
>   and Byways of the Yorkshire Dales

and:

>   Highways and Byways of the Yorkshire
>   Dales

Better still, however, are:

>   Highways and Byways
>   of the
>   Yorkshire Dales

Highways and
Byways of the
Yorkshire Dales

Highways and Byways of
the Yorkshire Dales

Where a book has a title and a subtitle the proper relation between them needs to be defined. Punctuation, such as a colon or a dash, usually looks ugly and should be avoided.

It is common for any special lettering or design work that has been done for the cover or jacket to be repeated on the title page. This helps provide an overall identity.

Title-page Verso Although this page is important for all the bibliographical data and so on that it contains, it is usually not a place which offers great opportunity for design. It is common for all the type on this page to be set in a size smaller than the text.

Lists of Contents, Illustrations, etc. The contents list is a vital piece of information in your publication and care needs to be taken to ensure its usefulness to readers. It is best to use more leading in the contents page than in the text for ease of reading. You should not need unsightly rows of dots, called 'dot leaders', to link the page numbers with the subject.

The layout is important to aid clarity. Chapter subheadings need to be differentiated from the main headings. A useful device, which also saves space in indexes, glossaries and lists in the text, is to use hanging indentation, with the first line full out and turnover lines and subheadings indented.

The 'drop' from the top of the page to the heading 'Contents' (not 'Contents List' or 'List of Contents') should be the same as the drop in the chapter headings. There is no need to use the word 'chapter' before the number of each chapter in the list.

Chapter Openings

The style devised for chapter openings should also be used for any foreword, preface, introduction or acknowledgements. Non-fiction books generally have chapter titles as well as numbers: titles should be more prominent than numbers. Whether you use Arabic, Roman or spelled-out numbers is entirely a matter of choice.

Non-fiction books of any reasonable length normally have each chapter starting on a fresh page. Preferably they should all start on a right-hand page. However, this may not be economical. If chapters are run on then a break of several lines needs to be left between one chapter and another. If there is room for less than (say) five lines of the new chapter at the foot of the page then the whole chapter should be carried over.

In books where chapters start on fresh pages there is usually a 'drop' of a number of lines before the chapter heading occurs. How long this drop should be may require some calculation if the chapter titles are very different in length and require setting on different numbers of lines.

A frequent device to make a new chapter look more impressive is to use a 'dropped' or 'cocked' initial. Examples of these are shown in Figure 5.12, pp.89–93.

In the days of hot metal typesetting, designers gave complicated instructions on how to mortise the letters by hand with a file to get the text close enough to dropped initials like A or L. This is usually a lot easier with modern imagesetting or DTP, but adjustment may still be necessary by hand with a scalpel, in which case some extra expense will be incurred. All dropped initials should be carefully examined on the proofs.

Another simple piece of design is to set one or more of the opening words of the chapter in capitals or small capitals. If this is done, then they look better if very thin spaces are inserted between the letters, called 'letter spacing'.

Some specimen chapter openings are shown in Figure 5.12, pp.89–93.

End Matter

Appendices are generally treated in the same way as chapters, although to save space they can be set in smaller type. Bibliographies, references, glossaries and indexes are usually set in smaller type, often with hanging indentation. Indexes are nearly always set in two (or more) columns, which saves a considerable amount of space. Other parts of the end matter can also be set in more than one column.

Figurative Matter

Figurative matter is the generic term for material which is set apart from the text for some reason. It covers diagrams, charts and other illustrative material, such as press cuttings or specimens, and tables.

You may have been provided with diagrams which are ready to be reproduced (known as 'camera-ready artwork'). The details of how you should process this are discussed in the next chapter, on pp.117–21. If you have only been provided with rough sketches or reference material, then you may have to commission someone to produce suitable artwork.

Commercial art studios will charge a lot of money to produce even the simplest diagram or chart, but if you brief them correctly then you should have no problems with it. When artwork is provided by someone who does not understand how to prepare material for reproduction, problems can arise. How you can avoid this is discussed in the next chapter, on pp.118–19.

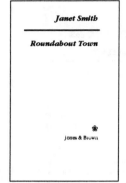

An example of a simple typographic design carried through the title page, prelims and chapter headings of a book. The rule and the display type add rhythm and consistency to the design.

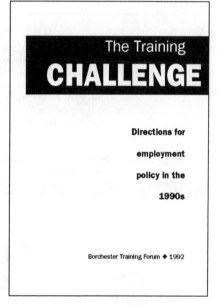

The title page sets the style for the whole book. The 'classical', symmetrical look may be restrained, but can be enlivened by the use of a decorative display type, used sparingly. An off-centre layout is often more appropriate for reports or other non-fiction. Again, the design can be spare and restrained – or more lively, as above.

Figure 5.12. Specimen pages.

Some styles for chapter openings. The use of letter spaced (often now called 'tracked') small capitals, drop or cocked initials are some ways of making an effective display. Use the longest chapter title to determine the style for the headings.

5: External relations since the coup

An elaboration and appraisal of the content and conduct of Ghana's foreign relations since the coup of 31 December 1981, must of necessity, be preceded by a look at what occurred before it. Nkrumah, who laid the foundations on which subsequent regimes were built, had a mixture of success and failure in foreign relations.

Florence by night

FLORENCE NIGHTLIFE has a relaxed and carefree mood that overrides the lack of an individual style. In recent years the club scene has come on leaps and bounds. Nearly all the clubs are in the city centre, and distances between them are on the whole walkable. And, of course, this being Italy and the centre of fashion, you have to look fashionable to gain entry to the most smart.

Public transport

Getting home after an all night rave is no problem since the buses run all through the night as well. So just relax

There were a king with a large jaw and a queen with a plain face on the throne of England; there were a king with a large jaw and a queen with a fair face on the throne of France. In both countries it was as clear as crystal to the Lords of the State preserves of loaves and fishes that things in general were settled for ever. It was the season of Light, it was the season of Darkness, it was the spring of hope, it was the winter of despair. We had everything before us, we had nothing before us, we were all going direct to Heaven, we were all going direct the other way – in short, the period was so far like the present period that some of its noisiest authorities insisted on its being received, for good or

Subheadings should occupy an exact number of text lines. If the text is on a 11pt body and the subheading is 13pt, occupying three lines of text, there will be 20pts over to distribute above and below it. The subheading should appear closer to the text that follows it rather than the text before, so in this case 14pts before and 6pts after is about right.

politics, some of his policies led to an irre breakdown in relations with a few neighbo especially Togo.

Foreign relations

◄ 14pt space

◄ 13pt subhead

◄ 6pt space

Along with such a decline in international influence, was a perceptible and devastatir stagnation of the national economy which analysts have blamed on Nkrumah's forei

Subheadings do not have to appear immediately above the text. In a book with wide margins, they can appear in the margins. In this case, because the text is ranged to the left, the subheadings look better if they are ranged right on both left and right-hand pages.

had a mixture of success and failure in foreign relations. While he succeeded in carving a central role for Ghana in African politics, some of his policies led to an irreparable breakdown in relations with a few neighbours, especially

Headlines (or running heads) should be differentiated from subheads. They often look best set in a small size of the text font in italic, or in letter spaced capitals. They can be separated from the text by a rule, or just by white space. In a design with wide margins the headline can be placed in the foredge. With an asymmetric layout, the folio can be incorporated into the headline, and should appear on the outside of the page. If the layout is centred, then the folio will probably need to be displayed separately.

breakdown in relations with a few West African neighbours, especially Togo. His fall in 1966, however, signalled the decline in Ghana's centrality and influence in both global and African politics. This was noted by Oteng in his 1969 monograph:

> Along with such a decline in international influence, was a perceptible and devastating stagnation of the national economy which some analysts have blamed on Nkrumah's preoccupation with foreign relations. As a result, post-Nkrumah regimes have had to prioritise basic national economic survival and have tended to relegate global affairs to the background. At the same time, however, the economic decline sharpened the need for foreign assistance, which increased Ghana's structural dependence and undermined its national autonomy.[3]

With the exception of the Acheampong regime, which briefly hit the headlines with its unprecedented call for the repudiation of Ghana's foreign debt, all post-Nkrumah regimes have pursued constrained and muted foreign relations and gave priority to domestic concerns. With the need for

Quoted matter should be differentiated from the rest of the text. The simplest way for this to be shown is by indenting from the left-hand margin, or both left and right-hand. It can also be set in a smaller size, or in italic or some other style. Lists can also be set in the same way, and points differentiated using asterisks, or some other device, such as bullet points:

If using these, find a design which does not clash awkwardly with the text typeface – a solid bullet point is sometimes rather strong for a delicate typeface.

the changes in which can be seen clearly in Table 6 below. The five year pattern has had a particularly bad effect on women's unemployment.

Table 6: Unemployment change in five London boroughs between 1979 and 1986.

	No.	%	No.	%	No.	%
UK	1,206,000	4.6	3,199,400	11.9	1,993,400	165.3
Greater London						
Camden	4,024	3.8	15,389	15.9	11,365	282.4
Greenwich	4,065	3.8	14,792	13.8	10,727	263.9
Hackney	5,258	5.7	20,527	22.3	15,269	290.4
Haringey	4,491	4.1	17,501	16.8	13,010	289.7
Islington	5,244	6.0	16,735	19.2	11,491	219.1
Five borough total	23,082	4.7	85,304	17.8	61,862	266.8

Source: Department of Employment

The 1981 recession also had a severe effect on the employment of black and other

A figure or table in the text should not be boxed in heavy rules or overlaid with a tint, if this can be avoided. If necessary, simple horizontal rules should be used. As with quoted matter, white space should be left above and below figurative matter.

Contents

Settings for lists of contents and other preliminary matter need not contain unsightly dot leaders (rows of dots). Here the page numbers are made obvious by ranging the chapter titles to the right and the folios to which they correspond to the left.

Commission for Racial Equality, *A Guide for Accommodation Agencies and Landlords* (London, CRE, 1982).

Department of the Environment, *Housing: the Government's proposals*, Cm 214 (London, HMSO, 1987).

Jones, Rita, *Landlord and Tenant Law*, 3rd edn (London, Legal and Eagle, 1988).

Singh, P K, *Housing Rights Guide*, (London, Housing Advice Centre, 1989).

Thompson, Harry, *UK Immigration Law in Practice*, (London,

Indexes, glossaries, bibliographies and other end matter can be set economically if 'hanging indentation' is used. In this the first line is set full out, and the second and subsequent lines are indented. The key word can be set in bold. If the end matter is set in two columns then a fairly small size of type can be used and it will take up even less space.

From a design point of view, it is important that figures are drawn both in an appropriate style and to the correct proportions. So if you are commissioning, say, a series of bar charts with lettering in position, specify the typeface that you want used to match your overall design.

Drawn figures are often produced bigger than the size at which they will be reproduced, as reduction in size diminishes any defects that might have occurred in the drawing. It is therefore important to specify exactly what size you want the figures to be, so that the artist can produce the artwork in the correct proportions. This can cause problems if you are not sure exactly where in the text you want the figures to go, or where you want several on the same page. You may need to do detailed layouts for individual pages to work out the correct size.

Computer Graphics Nowadays, computer software is widely available for the production of very high quality graphics which reproduce well in printing. This may be part of a DTP program or a piece of separate software. Use of this will obviously reduce the cost of artwork considerably.

Tables If you have followed the advice earlier (see p.55) then you should receive clearly typed and laid out tables. A specimen of a well-typed and presented table is shown in Figure 4.6 on p.54.

Marking up tables for the typesetter requires some careful thought but is not especially difficult. First of all, you should not be too frightened by a complicated typed table which looks as though it is going to take up an immense amount of space. A table which fits upright onto an A4 page when typed, even single spaced, will easily fit onto an A5 page when typeset. Even a typed table that has been 'turned' on the typed page may well fit upright when typeset. This is so because it is usual to set a table in smaller type than text (8pt is always legible and it is possible to go even smaller than that) and also because the proportional spacing used in typesetting is much more economical in tabular matter than fixed-space typing.

Try to ensure that all the tables in a book are set in the same size, unless they differ greatly in length. To work out the largest size possible in conventional typesetting, proceed as follows. (If you are doing your own artwork using DTP, trial and error on the largest table will probably be sufficient.)

Take the longest table and count the number of lines in it, including its heading and sources lines. Then decide the maximum depth you want this table to fill (this may be the depth of a page of text or may be less). Using a depth scale, work out which point size will allow you to fit your maximum number of lines inside this space. This should give you the size of body you can use for the type. Type in tables should preferably be leaded at least 1pt, and perhaps more, since this aids reading across the horizontal lines.

You do not have to work out the exact space to leave between the vertical columns in the table, since the typesetters will do this for you. But from your copyfitting tables (see Figure 5.11, p.84) you can tell how many characters will fill a line in the measure and size you have chosen. Count the maximum number of characters going across the longest line and add on two characters for each intercolumn space. If this comes to less than the number of characters given by the copy-fitting table then the table will fit. The typesetters will merely add intercolumnar space to drive out the table to the correct measure. If the table does not fit, then you can set it in a smaller size, or create more horizontal lines (if it is a non-numerical table), or as a last resort, turn it round on the page.

An example of the elegant design of a table is also shown in Figure 4.6, p.54. Note the very sparing use of rules – space is nearly always used to create the divisions for the eye to follow. It is usual to use bold or italic type for the vertical and horizontal axes.

Figurative Matter on the Page When considering how to set out figurative matter on the page, treat it as carefully as you would an illustration. The use of a grid, as discussed earlier in this chapter, should ensure that positions, margins and captions are consistent within the text. Pages and spreads should also be 'balanced' as much as possible, with care taken to avoid disruption to the readability of the text. Figurative matter in position on the page can be seen in the specimen page settings in Figure 5.12, pp.89–93.

Both illustrations and figurative matter should only be turned to a landscape shape as a last resort. If it is necessary, then the piece should be turned so that the top is on the outside on a left-hand page and on the inside on a right-hand page. If you are in the even more unhappy position of having tables or figures that are both turned and spread over a double page you should ensure that they go as far into the back as possible (allowing for the proposed binding process), so that they 'read' across the gutter.

Cover and Jacket Design

The cover or jacket of a book serves a different purpose from the text, and is therefore often designed differently. Its major function is to announce the title of the book and draw potential readers to it. It is first a marketing tool, the package in which your product has to compete in the marketplace, and then a source of information.

Designing for Impact

Your primary objective is to make a possible customer pick up your book and look at it. Market research shows that people decide within a few seconds of picking up a book whether to buy it or not, so if they select your book from what is offered to them, then you are halfway to a sale already!

Therefore your cover needs to make an impact. This may not necessarily be by means of an illustration. Simple effects, such as 'reversing out' type from a black or coloured background, can be used to make type more striking.

If you already have illustrations in your book then consider which of these would make the most eye-catching cover. Remember that the illustration on the cover serves a different purpose from that used inside, so try to think of a way of creating an impact. This could perhaps be done with an enlarged small detail, or an unusual halftone screen, or by using line instead of halftone, or by using extra colours. For more about treatment of illustrations, see pp.117–21.

The quality of the illustration used for the cover is very important, and this should be a factor in the one you choose if those used inside vary considerably in quality. A poor or damaged print will look a lot worse on a cover than it will inside.

House Style

If you produce a number of publications then you may want to consider producing them in an identifiable series or house style. This can be done in quite subtle ways, without cramming everything into a rigid grid. Virago, for instance, developed a distinctive house style by the use of a particular shade of green on virtually every cover, although the individual designs vary considerably. Similarly, Penguin publishes books which are immediately obvious as a series, yet its output is astonishingly diverse.

If you want to establish a series, then try to visualise any problems that might arise with future titles. For instance, if the first two books in your series are *Rights at Work* and *Rights in the Home,* then you might be tempted to go for a typographic treatment with the longest word set to the full width of the cover. But if a future title is to be *Rights at an Immigration Appeal Tribunal* then this might not be a very happy solution.

Spines

If your budget allows, and your book is long enough, then have it bound in a method which provides a spine. (See the section on binding methods, pp.141–4.) Your book will then be more readily identifiable on shelves. Type on the spine conventionally runs down, rather than up.

Overall Finish
Remember that a book left around in a shop does tend to get dirty, so avoid light coloured backgrounds, particularly if the cover is not protected by varnishing or lamination. The extra expense for protection by one of these methods (see p.144) is well worth the investment in ensuring that your book stays cleaner for longer on the shelves.

Information on the Cover
Basic information on the cover should always include the title and the author's name (both of which should be the same as on the title page), and a piece of selling copy, usually called a 'blurb'. You may or may not choose to print the price on the cover. If you do not, then you will need to have the facilities for labelling.

Most commercially published books also have other information, principally the International Standard Book Number (see p.29) and a bar code, which contains the price and ISBN in machine readable form, so that they can be read by a laser pen. Both of these are vital if you want to ensure commercial distribution for your title. WH Smith, for instance, will not take stocks of any title that does not have a bar code.

The bar code should be printed in a very dark colour on a pale background, otherwise the laser will not scan it properly. Black on white is preferable, but other dark colours such as blue and green also work well. Colours with a high proportion of red and yellow do not 'read' and should be avoided.

A full-size code can look rather unsightly, so ask your supplier for artwork for a bar width reduction of 20 microns and truncation of 45 per cent. This is what you will see on the back cover of this book.

The Publishers Association (listed in Useful Organisations, pp.148–9) can provide further information.

A number of suppliers can provide you with full details about how to get bar codes and supply artwork for them. One such is KTP Ltd, whose address can also be found in the Useful Organisations list on pp.148–9.

Sources
Simple books on design for the non-professional are hard to find. A few books that have been helpful are Ruari McLean, *The Thames and Hudson Manual of Typography* (London, Thames and Hudson, 1980), Douglas Martin, *An Outline of Book Design* (London, Blueprint, 1989), Oliver Simon, *Introduction to Typography*, 2nd edition, edited by David Bland (London, Faber and Faber, 1963), Alan Swann, *Basic Design and Layout* (Oxford, Phaidon, 1987) and *Pleasures of Design* (Cheltenham, Linotype, 1989). The copyfitting tables in Figure 5.11 are adapted from those in David Bann, *The Print Production Handbook* (London, Macdonald, 1986).

References
1. Beatrice Warde, *The Crystal Goblet* (London, Sylvan Press, 1955).
2. John Biggs, *The Use of Type* (London, Blandford Press, 1954).
3. Simon, *Introduction to Typography*.
4. McLean, *Typography*.

6

Typesetting, Proofs, Illustrations and Artwork Preparation

This chapter will take you through all the processes necessary to get your copy and illustrative material set out to your design and into the hands of the printers. It deals with typesetting, processing the proofs you receive from the typesetters and assembling all the text and illustrations in 'artwork', ready for the printers. Desktop publishing, which combines most of the elements of typesetting and artwork preparation, is dealt with in the next chapter.

Typesetting Systems

Even the most sophisticated of today's typesetting systems still use the Gutenberg principle of assembling words from individual letterforms. The difference, of course, is speed. Individual letterforms were once cast in metal in different sizes and styles and assembled by hand. Now they can be held in digital form in a computer's memory, produced in a variety of sizes and styles and assembled into words at the touch of a few keys.

Although computerised typesetting is the most common system used today, two other systems can still be found. All three are explained briefly below.

Hot-metal Setting
Mechanical typesetting was invented in the nineteenth century and considerably speeded up the cumbersome process of hand composition. There are two principal systems, the Monotype and the Linotype. On both, metal letters are cast in molten metal from a series of brass matrices, which are assembled by a machine after the operator types the text on a keyboard. The type can be used directly for printing by a letterpress printing machine or to provide 'repro' for artwork for offset litho machines. Repro (short for reproduction) is so called because a special hand-operated press is used to make high-quality prints suitable for photographing. The term is still sometimes used to describe artwork-quality setting generated by other systems.

Today's small publishers are unlikely to find hot metal setting economical (even when it is available). However, it can be argued that the craft of metal typography provides a yardstick for quality which no non-metal system yet devised can quite match.

Typewriters and Other 'Strike-on' Systems

The simplest method of all is the ordinary typewriter. Equipped with a carbon ribbon (to give a suitably black and even impression) an electric typewriter can give a perfectly usable image suitable for offset litho printing. Typewriters have the advantage of cheapness, speed and flexibility, and many small publishers have successfully produced many books and pamphlets in this way.

Until recently, the IBM Composer was frequently used for cheap text typesetting. In essence, this is little different from the electric golf-ball typewriter. It is rapidly becoming obsolete as desktop publishing becomes more widely used.

61. Our criticisms of the use of the present 'stop and search' powers have been made earlier (see paras. 17-20). We deplore the proposal of the Royal Commission on Criminal Procedure in its recent report (27) to extend these powers. Not only would the Commission's proposals extend the power to stop and search for stolen goods (which is now possessed by the Metropolitan Police and other large forces) to all parts of the country, but would extend the power itself to cover suspected possession of 'offensive weapons' and other prohibited items. We are opposed to the existence

Figure 6.1. Output from a daisywheel typewriter, reduced to approximately 70%. An ordinary electric typewriter or word processor printer can be used to provide an artwork-quality image, particularly if it is then reduced photographically.

Word processors are used more and more for the production of text. Correction or additions can be made easily without retyping whole pages or sections. A word processor may be used merely to speed up the production of drafts and to simplify the retyping and editing processes. If its output on paper is then used as artwork for litho printing, then there is no real difference in book production terms between it and the ordinary typewriter. But if the material typed in the word processor's memory is then used to produce the typesetting without being retyped, then this makes possible some different options. It also offers the chance for significant reductions in costs. The word-processed text can be converted to run through the typesetting machinery (a process usually called 'disk conversion') or can be imported directly into a desktop publishing program. Both are discussed further in Chapter 7.

Computerised Typesetting

The first British book entirely set on a computerised typesetting system and printed by offset litho was published as recently as 1957. In under 30 years the industry was totally transformed by these two processes which together gained complete ascendancy over typesetting in hot metal and printing by letterpress.

The first generation of photosetting equipment used a flash of light shone through photographic matrices of individual letters in order to produce an image on light-sensitive paper (often called a bromide). The latest imagesetters use laser technology to create the letterform on bromide paper or film.

In imagesetting, a digital version of the individual letter is stored by the machine at a very fine resolution (between 1,000 and 5,000 lines to the inch) and the shape of the letter is recreated first rather coarsely on a screen, for the operator to see, and then in a much finer version when output onto bromide or film. The resolution is so high that the human eye cannot detect that the letter is built up of dots. The revolutionary thing about imagesetting is that, for the first time in any typesetting system, the machine itself does not hold any images or matrices of the individual letterforms. The letterforms have, however, been used to create the digital information which the computer's memory contains. The Further Reading section, pp.150–3, contains details of books describing imagesetting in greater detail.

Some modern typesetting equipment is so sophisticated – and expensive – that it can produce completely made-up pages either as artwork, ready to be photographed, or as pieces of photographic film, from which litho plates can be made. Some have output that is little different from that produced by older systems, in that the page make-up and so on still has to be done by hand. The make-up of typesetting into pages is described on pp.111–13 and the process of making litho plates is described on pp.136–8.

If the typesetter is 'inputting' the text for you, operators will type it on a keyboard. They can usually see the typing on a visual display unit. Editing and corrections can be done at this time, but it is more common for the material to be stored, to be called up and edited or corrected later.

Figure 6.2. Simplified representation of the digitisation of a letterform. In fact, the letterform is stored in the computer's memory as a series of curves. The imagesetter or laser printer matches these curves as best it can with individual 'pixels', similar to those above. The higher the 'resolution' of the output device the more pixels there are, and hence the smoother the image becomes.

The operator also types in a number of commands along with the text. These vary according to the type of system in use, but they usually tell the machine the typeface, the style (roman, italic, bold, etc.), the size, the measure and the interlinear spacing (leading) and may also include end-of-line decisions about hyphenation, if the text is to be set justified.

The master program will also include functions such as kerning instructions, so that the space after letters with kerns such as T and f can be varied depending on the letter following them. A kern is the overhanging portion found on some letters (see Figure 5.6, p.70). The space after a letter T has to be greater when the letter following is, say, h than when the letter following is, say, e or o. The master program will also contain the digitised form of all the characters the machine is capable of setting.

These sophisticated typesetting systems offer advantages for the small publisher. Typesetting and printing costs have certainly not increased as fast as they might have done if the industry had remained wedded to metal. And many of the problems that were caused by the changeover from metal have been ironed out, though some remain. However it remains easy for the small publisher to be bamboozled by the jargon and apparent technical knowledge which seems to be necessary at this point, where the new technology has had its greatest effect on printing and publishing.

Although desktop publishing may seem to offer more control to the publisher it may not necessarily be the best way to proceed. The top DTP programs do indeed put in the hands of anyone the facilities previously only available to skilled professionals. But before taking on DTP at this level, the best advice must remain: think carefully about how you plan to use these facilities, and get proper training and back up.

Common Problems in Computerised Typesetting Despite many improvements over the first years of computerised typesetting, some disadvantages remain – even in today's latest generation imagesetters. It is as well to be aware of these. One is the poor quality of some type designs and the inadequate way in which some systems reproduce the designs at some sizes. Some designs are a travesty of the fine originals on which they are based. A good example of this is the Bembo typeface. In the 1920s the Monotype Corporation manufactured for hot metal setting a faithful reproduction of a fourteenth-century Italian typeface it called Bembo. Other versions of Bembo have now been produced, some of which can be seen and compared with the Monotype hot metal original in Figure 6.3, p.104. Even a casual glance will show that these versions do not measure up to the beautifully engraved quality of the Monotype version.

Even if the design is of adequate quality most systems use just one set of master drawings for reproducing all the sizes of a particular typeface. This is very poor practice, since the distortions necessary when a face is to be set in 8pt for footnotes are magnified when it is used in 72pt for display. The digitisation process in the latest generation of imagesetters reduces this problem. It is possible nowadays for the instructions for any particular character to be altered so that, say, the counters (enclosed part) of an e or an a can be kept more open in the smaller sizes than in the bigger sizes, to help rectify any distortion.

The other major problem is the inadequacy of automatic hyphenation and justification programs. Decisions about where to split words, which were previously made by an experienced, literate human being, are now made by a computer. The program may contain an exception dictionary so that logical rules for the machine to follow, such as 'break between two consonants' can be varied to allow exceptions such as debt-or, fea-ther, wash-able. These dictionaries are often not as detailed as one might wish and words are often broken in completely the wrong place – I have recently seen, for example, somew-here and Londo-ners.

A good explanation of the change is made by Cynthia Cockburn, in her book *Brothers*, an interesting study of the impact of new technology on the lives of male typesetters:

We have equalized our

Dexterity in the

ABCDEFGHIJKMN

New Patterns 1950-1980

Early History II, to 1820

Detention and
Release

Figure 6.3. Examples of Bembo typeface produced by different typesetting systems. The top example is Monotype hot metal, the lower examples are from various computerised typesetting systems.

Some men feel that they are ... trying to maintain the standards to which they are accustomed in the face of indifference all round. 'I get the feeling that I'm not supposed to be concerned with quality any more but quantity.' An instance of this is that end-of-line decisions produced by the computer's limited programs are inferior to those devised by the judgement of an experienced operator... As a Linotype operator the [typesetter] knew, remembered and observed a set of rules for splitting words. He had to be ready to decide when to 'turn the line over', how to deal with word breaks, how much white space was tolerable between words. This decision-making influenced his setting from the first character of the line till the last.[1]

Too often, the publisher is now presented with little alternative to poor type design, bad word breaks and gappy setting. Small publishers with little economic muscle are not the only people to suffer this – major book, magazine and newspaper publishers are often plagued with the same problems. We can only hope that the latest generation of imagesetters can adapt and improve to reach a level of excellence equivalent to the technology which they are replacing. This, to quote Hugh Williamson in *Methods of Book Design*, will only occur if

> publisher and printer equally assert by their actions that no lower standards will be offered or accepted in the long term ... If [the typesetter's] initiative is now to be delegated to electronic machinery, the improvements of five hundred years, devised for manual typography and hardly affected by mechanical typesetting, may be found economically inconvenient.[2]

Proofs and Proofreading

Proofs are the various kinds of test impressions made at different stages of the production process to give you some idea of what the final job will look like and to provide an opportunity to correct mistakes and make alterations. It is normal to get proofs of typesetting at its various stages, and also of the printing if the job involves colour or a lot of illustrations. The more advanced the process has become the more expensive it is to correct proofs, so it is always advisable to ensure that the original material is accurate, to make only necessary changes and to make them at the earliest possible stage.

Later on, we will deal with the proofing processes which occur during printing. Here we are concerned with typesetting proofs.

Proofs of typesetting normally come in two forms, galley proofs and page proofs. The first kind, called after the long trays in which metal type was stored after it was set, is now normally a photocopy of the paper copy generated by the typesetting processor. After these are corrected then the text and any illustrations, captions, headings and other material are assembled into representations of the pages of your book or pamphlet, which are again copied for your inspection, and called 'page proofs'. Sometimes the galley proof stage is omitted altogether, particularly in simple books without illustrations.

Alterations at both galley and page proof stage are expensive and should be restricted, if possible, to the correction of errors. The author receives a proof only to check that the typescript has been followed correctly. However, authors are human and the fact that the text is now available to them in a fresh, new form may sometimes make the desire for other changes irresistible. To avoid this, it should be made clear to them that only essential changes should be made. In commercial publishing, authors may be charged for non-essential corrections.

If you are planning to go through both stages, galley and page proofs, it is a good idea to send the author the galley proofs only. The author should be able to do all her or his corrections at this stage and you can use the page proof yourself only to check that the corrections have all been done and that all the other elements have been assembled correctly.

Some, but not all, typesetters employ readers to check proofs against the typescript. If this is so, then one set of proofs may arrive in your hands as a 'marked set' with some corrections and queries already marked. This you should retain and proofread yourself, so send another copy to the author, with any queries that only she or he can answer marked on it. When you receive the author's set back then you should collate them with your corrections onto the marked set.

Ideally, you should use a system of colour-coding the corrections to proofs. Alterations which you or the author make are all known as 'author's corrections' and should be marked in blue. Typesetters' errors should be marked in red. The typesetters' proofreaders will have already used green to mark corrections they have noticed. You should then only be charged for corrections marked in blue.

How to Read Galley Proofs

Small publishers can rarely afford the additional cost of employing a freelance proofreader, so it is quite likely that you will have to read the proofs yourself. It is a good idea to read a separate proof from the one you have sent your author since you may pick up more errors between the two of you. If an error has already been marked then it is quite easy to miss another close to it.

Proofreading means unlearning all the habits you have developed to read and make sense of a piece of writing. Quick readers read a phrase at a time and disregard spelling and other errors. Train yourself to read proofs slowly, seeing every letter in every word and noting the punctuation of every sentence. You may find it easier to notice errors if you use a ruler or a piece of paper to ensure that you only read a line at a time.

You may be reading against the copy, which means checking the proof against the typescript a line or a sentence at a time, or you may be only reading 'for sense'. If you have time you should do both! Occasionally, proofs are still checked against copy using a 'copyholder', who reads the typescript out loud in full, mentioning all punctuation, capitalisation, italicisation, etc., to the proofreader. This is a quick method if another person is available and is certainly to be recommended if there is a lot of detailed work. Magazines which publish knitting patterns, for instance, usually use two sub-editors to check proofs this way.

If you are proofreading a book you have already copy-edited you will find it useful to refer to the style sheet (see p.32) for unusual spellings, hyphenation, etc. If the book is new to you then mark any optional forms with a highlighter or a marginal pencil mark. It will then be quicker to go back through the proofs later to check for consistencies.

In *Copy-editing*, Judith Butcher supplies some useful tips:

- If there is a glaring error, one's eye tends to leap over the intervening words; so when you have marked the correction then read the whole line again.
- Obvious misspellings are relatively easy to spot but errors which change one word to another are more likely to slip through: causal for casual, ingenuous for ingenious and (commonly) now for not.
- On the other hand the author may have deliberately used an unusual word – so the slightly different word may not be wrong.
- Do not alter inconsistent spelling, capitalisation, etc. in quotations.
- Check particularly the things the author may take for granted: prelims, headings, headlines and numerical sequences such as page numbers, notes and note identifiers, sections, figurative matter, etc.

How to Mark Corrections

Proofreading corrections must be marked in both the text and the margin, as the typesetter looks in the margin for lines or sections that need to be corrected. This differs from editing marks which are only marked in the text. A mark in the text only may be overlooked. The correction should be in the margin nearer to the error, level with the error and finished with an oblique stroke. If the line contains more than one error then the corrections should be written in the order they appear, left to right, separated by oblique strokes.

There is a British Standard series of proof correction marks (BS 5261) summarised in Figure 6.4, pp.108–11. However, by no means all of these marks are in common use yet (despite the fact that they were introduced in 1976!) so you may come across some alternative marks.

Some further points:

- Ring full points and colons for clarity.
- Distinguish commas and quotation marks carefully.
- If you delete a letter or letters, make it absolutely clear which are being deleted. Carelessly written diagonal strokes can pass through correct neighbouring letters.
- Do not also use a delete mark if you are substituting new words or letters. The insertion mark and the new material are sufficient.
- Do not try to be too clever by saving the odd word or phrase in a rewritten sentence. By the time the typesetter has followed your train of thought she or he could have reset the whole sentence.
- If you are correcting an unusual word write the correct spelling of the whole word in the margin next to the correction and ring it.
- Keep a set of coloured fine point pens specially for proof correcting.

Instruction	Textual mark	Marginal mark
Leave unchanged	‑ ‑ ‑ ‑ under characters	⊘
Remove extraneous marks	Encircle marks to be removed	✕
Delete	/ through character(s) or ⊢⊣ through words	℘
Delete and close up	⌒ through character(s) or ⊟	℘
Insert in text the matter indicated in the margin	⅄	New matter followed by ⅄
Substitute character or substitute part of one or more word(s)	/ through character or ⊢⊣ through word(s)	New character or new word(s)
Substitute ligature e.g. ffi for separate letters	⊢⊣ through characters affected	⊂ e.g. ffi
Substitute or insert full stop or decimal point	/ through character or ⅄	⊙
Substitute or insert comma, semi-colon, colon, etc.	/ through character or ⅄	,/ ;/ ⨀ ⸔/
Substitute or insert character in 'superior' position	/ through character or ⅄	⅄ under character e.g. ²⅄
Substitute or insert character in 'inferior' position	/ through character or ⅄	⅄ over character e.g. ⅄₂
Substitute or insert single or double quotation marks or apostrophe	/ through character or ⅄	⸚ ⸚ and/or ⸛ ⸛
Substitute or insert ellipsis	/ through character or ⅄	•••
Substitute or insert hyphen	/ through character or ⅄	⊢⊣
Substitute or insert rule	/ through character or ⅄	Give the size of the rule in the marginal mark e.g. ⊢1em⊣ ⊢4mm⊣
Substitute or insert oblique	/ through character or ⅄	⊘
Wrong fount. Replace by character(s) of correct fount	Encircle character(s)	⊗
Change damaged character(s)	Encircle character(s)	✕

Figure 6.4. British Standard Series proof correction marks.

Instruction	Textual mark	Marginal mark
Set in or change to italic	——— under character(s). Where space does not permit textual marks encircle the affected area instead	 ⊔⊔⌋
Change italic to upright type	Encircle character(s)	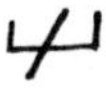 ⌶⌋
Set in or change to capital letters	≡ under character(s)	≡
Set in or change to small capital letters	= under character(s)	=
Set in or change to bold type	∿∿ under character(s)	∿∿
Set in or change to bold italic type	 ∿∿ under character(s)	 ⊔⊔⌋ ∿∿
Change capital letters to lower-case letters	Encircle character(s)	≢
Change small capital letters to lower-case letters	Encircle character(s)	≠
Invert type	Encircle character	↻
Close up. Delete space between characters or words	linking  ⌒ characters	 ⊃
Insert space between characters	∣ between characters	Y. Give the size of the space when necessary
Insert space between words	Y between words	Y. Give the size of the space when necessary
Reduce space between characters	∣ between characters	⊤. Give the amount by which the space is to be reduced when necessary
Reduce space between words	�⊤ between words	 ⊤. Give the amount by which the space is to be reduced when necessary
Make space appear equal between characters or words	∣ between characters or words	 ⋎
Close up to normal interline spacing	(each side of column) linking lines	

Instruction	Textual mark	Marginal mark
Insert space between lines or paragraphs	or	Give the size of the space when necessary
Reduce space between lines or paragraphs	or	Give the amount by which the space is to be reduced when necessary
Start new paragraph		
Run on (no new paragraph)		
Transpose characters or words	between characters or words, numbered when necessary	
Transpose lines		
Transpose a number of lines	3 2 1	Rules extend from the margin into the next with each line to be transposed numbered in the correct sequence
Centre	enclosing matter to be centred	[ ]
Indent		Give the amount of the indent
Cancel indent		
Set line justified to specified measure*	and/or	
Set column justified to specified measure*		
Move matter specified distance to the right*	enclosing matter to moved to the right	
Move matter specified distance to the left*	enclosing matter to be moved to the left	
Take over character(s), word(s) or line to next line, column or page		The textual mark surrounds the matter to be taken over and extends into the margin

Instruction	Textual mark	Marginal mark
Take back character(s), word(s) or line to previous line, column or page	⌐⎯⎯⎯⎯⏋	The textual mark surrounds the matter to be taken back and extends into the margin
Raise matter*	⤒ over matter to be raised ⎺⎺⎯⎯⎯⎯⎽ under matter to be raised	⎤⎽⎽⎽⎽⎡
Lower matter*	⎽⎽⎽⎽⎤ over matter to be lowered ⤓ under matter to be lowered	⎽⎯⎯⎯⎯⎤
Move matter to position indicated*	Enclose matter to be moved and indicate new position	
Correct vertical alignment	‖	‖
Correct horizontal alignment	Single line above and below misaligned matter	⎯⎯⎯⎯ ⎯⎯⎯⎯ placed level with the head and foot of the relevant line

*Give the exact dimensions when necessary

Making Up Pages from Galleys

The process of turning the typeset galleys into the pages of a book is still often done by hand, particularly if the book is heavily illustrated (although you may be doing your own pages using DTP, or your type-setters may have computerised page make-up facilities).

If you have never done it before, think carefully before you decide to produce your own completely finished artwork. You may find it difficult to do accurately and it could be expensive if the printers have to make alterations before they can use it.

If you have used an experienced designer then he or she will probably do the artwork for you and you should not have any technical problems with the printers.

If you have designed the text yourself and you want the typesetters to make up the artwork then you should provide them with a rough paste-up of a set of galley proofs to follow. You should do this, if possible, on copies of your design grid, preferably as 'spreads' so that you can see each opening of the book as it will finally look. If your book is an A4 format then you will need A3 copying facilities to get

When you talk to a comp about the newspaper, he expresses no surprise if you suggest that the product is something that has political and ideological significance in class terms. He is quick to say, himself, for instance, that his paper is an 'establishment paper'. He may say, 'It puts about ideas that are damaging to trade unions' or, in the the case of the *Daily* Mirror, 'they claim to take a working-class view but...' He recognizes that the ownership of the paper is significant, that a newspaper confers its owners and makes wealth (when it is properly managed) for the corporation that invests in it. Try, however, suggesting to him that the paper he produces is political and ideological from another point of view in that it confers political power on men. The compositor will look at you in surprise.

Yet newspapers are an important part of the processes by which the hegemony of masculist ideas and values is sustained. male rivalry, competitiveness and prowess are given a daily boost in the sports, war and crime reporting. There is a strident assumption that the reader is heterosexual, with the matching assumption that if you are not you are a misfit. The family, with its paraphernalia of love, marriage and babies (royal and common) is a subject of cartoons, such as Andy Capp. The double standard fills the continual celebration, but its contradictions crop up painfully in the tabloids: here a chat piece with a bereaved mother, there a full-page nude in leather boots. As Anna Coote and Beatrix Campbell have pointed out, 'during the 1970s...the idea of a "newspaper" became inseparable, in the minds of many millions of British readers, from the idea of naked female breasts.' Page 3 of *The Sun*, with its huge photos of 'lovelies', 'dazzlers', 'sizzlers' and 'tantalisers', has become a catchword in musical comedy and offstage.

From *Brothers* by Cynthia Cockburn.

Figure 6.5. Corrected galley proof.

your double-page grid on a single sheet. Make plenty of copies of your grid since you are bound to make some mistakes.

A rough paste-up of the galleys should be done from an unmarked set of proofs. The marked set should be returned with the paste-up. The typesetters will insert all the corrections and then make up the pages from the corrected version.

Obviously, there may be problems if the galley corrections mean that the text is altered in length. If this is so, then you should try to compensate for this when doing the paste-up so that, for instance, if five lines of text have been cut on a page then you allow for this by adding in a compensatory five lines while pasting up. This can been seen more fully in Figure 6.6, p.114.

Cut round the galleys close to the type area and paste them onto the grids using wax, Cow Gum or Spraymount (in a well-ventilated place), since these adhesives enable you to move things around more easily if you change your mind or make a mistake.

Doing Your Own Artwork

Equipment
If you decide to paste up your own artwork you will find it a lot easier with a small amount of specialist equipment, which you can find in any graphic or artist's supplies shops. What people find most useful varies from person to person, but what I use is the following:

- Scalpel blades and blade holder. Swann-Morton 10a blades are the most useful shape. They fit into a No. 3 holder.
- Steel straightedge or ruler. It is worth buying a metal typescale which you can then use both for cutting against and for measuring type.
- Clear plastic ruler embossed with a parallel line grid. An 18 inch or 24 inch ruler is useful, since you may need to draw accurate lines longer than 12 inch.
- Suitable adhesive. The aerosol Spraymount is often used, but can be rather messy and is dangerous to health if your workplace is not well ventilated. Professional studios use hot wax, but the cheapest hand-held dispensers cost over £50. Cow Gum (a rubber solution, not made from cows!) is often regarded as old fashioned, but I find it the simplest substance to use, especially if it is applied from a tin, not a tube, with a thin metal artist's palette knife rather than the plastic dispenser made by the manufacturer.
- Large set square. Either 45 or 60 degrees will do.
- Light-blue pencil. For drawing lines on artwork which will not show up when it is photographed by the printer. Do not go to the expense of buying special 'non-reproducing' pencils – any light-blue crayon will suffice.

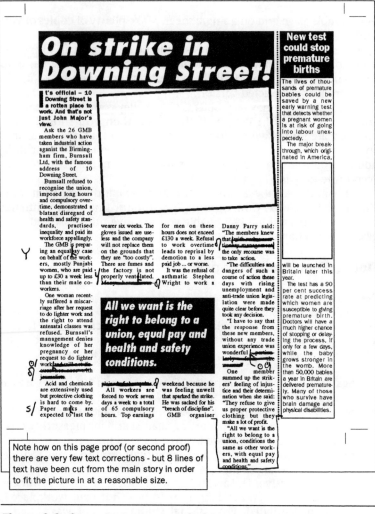

Figure 6.6. Corrected page proof of a magazine, showing how text cuts have been made to compensate for overmatter.

- Very fine steel-tipped black pen, with a 0.1 or 0.2 mm point. There are plenty of inexpensive pens on the market which are just as good for occasional work as specialist refillable drawing pens. These are expensive, usually messy to fill and tiresome to keep clean.
- White-out fluid. Preferably a new bottle with a nice fine brush!

With these tools, a decent flat table, some plain white heavy card and scrap paper, you should be able to manage any paste-up. A specialist self-healing cutting mat is not essential but is quite useful, since it can be used as a base on which to work on your table.

Designers usually use a drawing board with a parallel motion in order to produce accurate squared-up artwork. You do not need to obtain such an expensive piece of equipment if you are only going to do small amounts of work, but you might want to consider it.

How to Paste Up

The most important thing about paste-up is to get everything straight and squared up. In order to ensure accuracy, professional designers will often get accurate grids preprinted in pale blue for them to paste onto. You might like to consider this if you have a large book to do. Alternatively you can purchase preprinted grids in standard formats such as A4 and A5 from some designers and printers. If you are going to use a standard grid, plan your design around it.

For a short book or pamphlet it will probably be sufficient to draw up your own grids in light-blue pencil on plain white card. You can also paste up onto heavy tracing paper (available in art shops) so you can draw up grids more quickly by tracing them off a master copy. The edge of the page should be signified by corner marks drawn in fine black pen. A typical grid can be seen in Figure 6.7, p.116.

Your paste-up can be done as spreads to appear the way they will appear in the final book or pamphlet – in other words, with p.2 facing p.3, and so on. The printers will make them up to the correct 'imposition' to fit their printing and binding machinery. For more about imposition, see p.136.

The typematter which you are going to paste up will probably be in galley form. Before beginning the paste-up of each spread, cut out the typematter for each page from the galley with a scalpel and steel rule, leaving a small margin (about 3 to 5mm) around the edges. Any other elements for the spread which have been set or supplied separately, such as headlines, chapter headings, subheadings, illustrations or figurative matter, should also be cut out.

Place all the matter down 'dry' on the grid, to check everything fits and then begin the paste-up from the top of the page. Place each piece to be pasted in turn upside down onto scrap paper and ensure the adhesive is spread evenly in a thin film up to each edge. Pick up the pasted piece carefully with the spreader and place it onto the grid in the correct position. Adhesives such as Cow Gum, Spraymount or wax do not solidify immediately, so the piece can be moved around for about 30 seconds, which gives you time to check whether it is positioned and squared up correctly with a ruler with a parallel line grid or a set square. When the piece is accurately positioned, place a piece of plain white paper over it and gently press it down to the surface.

If you make a mistake, don't worry. You can lift pieces off the surface for up to about 10 minutes by prising them gently away with a palette knife. After this time, you may need to soften the adhesive by flooding the area with some petrol lighter fuel, which is sold for this purpose in art supply shops. Don't smoke while doing this!

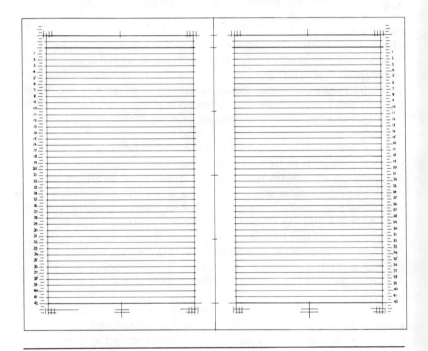

Figure 6.7. Typical grid for paste-up. This is for a Demy Octavo book, 216 x 138mm.

When you have finished each grid, clean up any marks either with a little lighter fuel on a tissue or with a little ball of solidified Cow Gum, which pulls any surplus gum off the surface. Use white-out fluid to cover anything that won't clean off in this way.

This description of paste-up is rather brief. Once you have tried it, you will find that it is largely a mixture of practice and confidence – plus the ability to see whether what you have done looks both straight and squared up. Further information can be found in a number of books listed under Sources at the end of this chapter.

Illustrations

If your book contains illustrations, or figurative material, then you will now have to make final decisions about what goes where, and in what size. You may have already done this when planning your design – or you may have been collecting illustrative and figurative material without making detailed plans.

The next section deals with how to prepare illustrative and figurative material for reproduction and how to mark it to the correct size.

Originals for Reproduction

The better the quality of the originals from which your printers reproduce, the better will be the result. This may seem obvious but it is often the case that inexperienced small publishers provide printers with poor quality originals and then are disappointed with the results.

Illustrative material is produced in two ways. 'Line' material has no intermediary tones between black and white and is photographed directly by the camera used to make negatives for platemaking. Material with changes in tone (usually photographs, but also pencil or crayon drawings) is reproduced by converting it into patterns of dots of different sizes corresponding to the changes in density of the lines in the original. This process is called making a 'halftone' and involves rephotographing the original through a regular fine mesh of dots called a 'screen'.

The halftone process is used either to make a piece of negative film, which is itself used to make a litho plate, or a positive 'screened photomechanical transfer' (PMT) print which is pasted into the rest of the artwork from which a negative and then a litho plate are made. See Figure 6.8, p.118, and p.121 for more about photomechanical transfer prints.

Line Originals

Drawings, diagrams, etc. should be drawn in black ink on a white background. Reduction in size often minimises any inaccuracies so they are often drawn bigger than the final size. Pencil or other grey shading should never be added to the original but should be simulated either by pen-drawn hatching or a 'mechanical' adhesive tint such as Letratone.

If you are printing in two or more colours, then any overlapping colour areas must be supplied to the printers as separate pieces of artwork, each drawn in black ink and not in the colour it is to appear in. Artists who are experienced in drawing for reproduction should be used to this technique but others may not be, so this may need to be explained to them.

The second or any subsequent colours should be drawn in black on an acetate film or tracing paper overlay, with accurate register marks

Photograph 'screened' through a process camera to produce a photomechanical transfer (PMT) print with a pattern of dots of different sizes, called a 'halftone'. Here, the screen has 85 lines per inch, and the dots are easily visible to the naked eye. When the screened print is further enlarged (left) the way in which the dots differ in size between light and dark parts of the original is clearly visible.

The PMT process can also be used for other effects, such as reversing type out of a solid or tinted background (left) or out of a photograph (as simulated right). When reversing type ensure both that the type is bold enough and the background dark enough to maintain legibility.

Figure 6.8. Halftone screens, and other effects produced by the PMT process.

drawn on both the base and the overlay. The printer will make a separate negative and plate from each piece of artwork and can ensure that the colours fit together accurately. See Figure 6.9, opposite.

Line material such as newspaper cuttings should be of as high quality as possible. Good, high-contrast photocopies may be adequate. Each piece of material of this kind should be lightly glued (using an adhesive that does not discolour, such as Spraymount, Cow Gum or Pritt) to separate pieces of white paper.

Base drawing to be printed in black. Note the register marks, drawn away from the image area.

Overlay for printing in blue. The colour runs up to the edges of the clouds so that they appear white.

Overlay for printing in red. Because a Letratone tint has been put on the on the smock area, this will appear pink.

Figure 6.9. Line drawing with separate overlays for each colour.

Halftones

Photographs to be reproduced as halftones should be high-quality black and white prints with good contrast and detail. It is possible to reproduce colour prints in black and white but the results will not be very satisfactory. Again, prints that are slightly bigger than the final size will usually give better results.

Drawings in pencil or crayon or other media which have intermediary tones between black and white can be reproduced as halftones. This usually means that the background to the drawing will appear as a light tint of black. If the drawing is suitable the camera operator may be able to 'drop out' this tinted background so that it appears white. An example of how this has been done can be seen in Figure 6.10, p.120.

Figure 6.10. Crayon drawing screened as a halftone.

You can, of course, use only part of the detail of a photograph. The area to be used should be marked either on a tracing paper overlay attached to the print or on a photocopy.

Other Special Effects

The cameras and platemaking equipment used by printers can be used to create other sophisticated effects. A line negative and a halftone negative can be used in platemaking so that, for example, type can be superimposed on a photograph. Similar processes are used to create tints, 'reversals' and other effects (see p.137).

A 'duotone' can add a pleasing lustre to photographs if a second colour is being used in the printing. In this process two halftones of the same original are produced and printed in separate colours on top of each other. By varying the density at which the coloured halftone is produced a whole range of effects become available. This cannot be demonstrated in this book – as there is no second colour – but can often be seen in other books and magazines.

Colour can also be used to highlight detail in a halftone – for instance to create joke effects like a red nose.

Photomechanical Transfer (PMT) Prints

A process known as photomechanical transfer (PMT) is often used to produce screened halftone prints, reduced or enlarged to the correct size, which can then be pasted directly onto the artwork. This means that photographs do not have to be turned separately into screened negatives and stripped in with the line negatives of the text. The printers can make a single negative from the whole artwork, both line and halftone.

The PMT process is also often used to make line prints to the right size and for special effects, such as 'reversing out' type, that is making it appear as white on a black background.

If you are using correct size PMT prints of your illustrations then you do not need to send the original material to the printers. You will also see all the halftones in place on the final artwork.

Many high street 'instant printers' can supply you with PMT prints.

Marking the Sizes for Reproduction
If you have access to a photocopier with zoom reduction and enlargement then the process of marking the sizes for both halftone and line material is very easy. You can use the copier to make copies to the size you want, crop them and tack them lightly onto your rough paste-up. Then you mark the same percentage reduction or enlargement you have used on the originals. Mark photographs on the reverse (in very soft pencil or crayon) and line material in its margin. The copies should only be lightly tacked down since you may need to transfer them later to either the final page proofs or the artwork.

If you do not have a zoom photocopier (or a process camera for making PMTs) the position of an illustration is normally marked by a rectangle drawn to the final size. This shape and size is calculated by constructing a rectangle of the same proportion as the original from its diagonal. This is shown in Figure 6.11, p.122. An overlay can be used to give sizing instructions to the printers.

Any illustrative material to be reproduced the same size should be simply marked 's/s'.

Finally, all originals for illustrative material should be lettered or numbered and the corresponding letters or numbers used in the paste-up.

Page Proofs

If the typesetters have made up artwork following your rough paste-up then all you have to do with page proofs is to check that typesetting corrections have been made and that all the other components fit together as you planned them.

There should be no need to read through the text again. However, you should read to the end of every paragraph that has been corrected to ensure that a mistake has not been made later on. You should also ensure that all corrected lines have been inserted in the right place.

If you did not give the typesetters an exact paste-up of your own – or if you have used a designer – then there may be other matters

Left: the photograph or illustration to be used.
Above: the space available on the layout.

Trace the shape you have available onto tracing paper, and draw a diagonal from the bottom left through the top right corner to the edge of the paper. Alternatively, make a photocopy of the picture and draw the shape and diagonal on the photocopy.

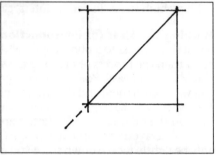

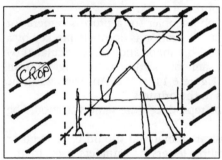

Place the tracing paper over the photograph and decide which parts of it you want to include. Using your diagonal, ensure that these fall within an area of the same proportions as the space you have available. Trace some of the photograph's features for the printer to follow as a guide, and draw a box to show the exact area to be reduced. Cross out the areas to be cropped.

You now know the height and width of the area of the photo you want to use and the height and width of the space you have available. Calculate the percentage by which the photo must be reduced to fit the space. Or simply mark the final size, both height and width.

The same procedure can be used for enlarging illustrative material.

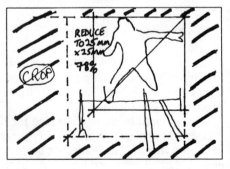

Figure 6.11. Diagonal method for sizing illustrative material.

If you did not give the typesetters an exact paste-up of your own – or if you have used a designer – then there may be other matters which you should check.

Try to avoid 'widows' (short lines at the top of a page or column) and 'orphans' (short lines at the foot of a page or column). You may need to do this by cutting or adding a few words further back in the paragraph. If you have to do this, make this correction as near to the end of the paragraph as possible.

Similarly, the designer may want you to 'save' or 'make' some lines, so that the design fits together better.

Check the page numbers (folios), that the footnotes are on the correct pages, that headings and headlines are correct.

Insert the missing page numbers into the contents list and any lists of illustrations or figurative matter and check the captions against the list as a final precaution.

Insert or check page numbers in cross references.

If any page numbers are incorrect then ensure that any set of page proofs being used for indexing is also altered.

If you do not need to send the page proofs to the author then do not do so. This may not be practical, however, if your book is complicated and you need her or him to approve the illustrations and the layout of the pages. But stress that only vital corrections should be made at this stage.

Final Checking

If you are not pasting up the artwork yourself then all there is left for you to do is to stick either the correct-size photocopies of the illustrations, or rectangles representing them, on a photocopy of the final artwork of the typematter (rather than on the artwork itself) and send it to the printers, along with the originals of the illustrations. (If the illustrations were supplied to the printers as correct-size PMTs already in position, then this is not necessary.)

Whatever route you have used to get to this stage, this is the very last time that you will see your book before it is printed. So check your artwork or final page proofs very carefully indeed, paying particular attention to such obvious things as the title page and chapter headings. It is better to waste a little time now, sending it back to the typesetter or designer, rather than letting a glaring error creep through because of an oversight.

Sources

Two books provide very helpful information on typesetting and origination methods. They are David Bann, *The Print Production Handbook* (London, Macdonald, 1986) and Hugh Williamson, *Methods of Book*

Design, 3rd edition (London, Yale University Press, 1983). Both also contain full glossaries.

How to paste up your own artwork is covered in Jonathan Zeitlyn, *Effective Publicity and Design* (London, Journeyman Press, 1992), and John Laing (editor), *Do-it-yourself Graphic Design* (London, Ebury Press, 1984).

References
1. Cynthia Cockburn, *Brothers: Male Dominance and Technological Change,* 2nd edition (London, Pluto Press, 1991).
2. Williamson, *Methods of Book Design.*

7

Desktop Publishing

Introduction

The first thing to be said about desktop publishing is that it has an inaccurate name: it is only part of the publishing process. It would, in fact, be better described as desktop typesetting and artwork production, since conventional printing and binding is still needed to produce a book from the output of a DTP system.

Secondly, despite the impression you might gain from advertising, the cost of the computer equipment and software you will need to produce typesetting and artwork of a standard approaching the professional will be high – perhaps £4,000 in all, at 1992 prices. That is a lot of money to invest if you are only planning to produce a small number of publications. (Your output will still only be of the quality of a high-class photocopier. To produce print quality of professional standard you will have to buy an imagesetting processor – a further investment of thousands of pounds.) Of course, you may be planning to use the computer or printer hardware for other functions, but you will still need special software and possibly a high-resolution monitor.

The final caveat is the one that is probably mentioned the least. Design and typesetting can be learned, but they require study and practice. Anyone who thinks they can produce material without either will probably end up with something that looks shoddy and amateur. However, these skills can be developed – and one of the purposes of this book is to help you do just that.

The advance of DTP has given many people the chance to try their hand at design and typesetting – and given them access to facilities which allow them more control over the process of getting into print. That can only be a good thing.

This chapter is not a step-by-step guide to producing material on DTP. That process should be explained properly in the official manual that accompanies your software or in a specialist guidebook for the program. (If the manual is not adequate then the software is probably not adequate either!)

What follows is more a brief general discussion of what DTP is and what it can do. The actual processes of design, typesetting and page make-up are described in other places in this book. Some further information can be found in the Sources section at the end of this chapter.

What is Desktop Publishing?

DTP is the generic name for computer software programs in which simple text, typed into a computer as for word processing, is arranged on a page in columns, and in different sizes and styles. These sizes and styles are based on those used in conventional typesetting. Photographs, illustrations and figurative material can be scanned, inserted and altered in size and shape.

The actual software varies from program to program, but that is its essence. At the top end of the range, DTP programs are now used by professional editors, designers and typesetters.

The output is usually first printed out on a laser dry-toner printer, which uses a method similar to that of a photocopier. This provides quite good quality artwork but not as good as that from an imagesetter outputting onto bromide paper or photographic film. Professional quality programs can also use a more sophisticated laser imagesetter, which produces true artwork quality material.

The difference in 'quality' of the program is governed by the quality of the digitisation of the typefaces and other images used and whether the program uses a page description language, such as PostScript. (Digitisation of typefaces is discussed on pp.101–3. Page description language is explained on p.128.)

Figure 7.1, opposite, shows how the output from an imagesetter compares with that from a laser printer. Most laser printers produce images scanned at about 300 dots per inch (dpi), although 600 dpi is now available. An imagesetter's scanning is at a much higher resolution – at least 1500 dpi, and usually more.

Many more publishers are, however, choosing to use laser printers for the production of their final artwork. The reason is of course cost, since laser-printed output on plain paper costs just pennies a page, compared with several pounds per page for output on film or bromide from an imagesetter.

This book, as I am sure a perceptive reader will have noticed already, is printed from laser output. The text typeface, Stone Serif, was designed by the American typographer Sumner Stone especially for DTP use and laser printing.

If you do not want to acquire your own imagesetter you will easily find typesetting bureaux which will output your material. If you want to print your books or pamphlets by litho, and you are contemplating doing the typesetting and design on a DTP system, then you may well find that this is the most satisfactory way of getting artwork of a high enough quality.

Ae 12 **A3** 72pt.

ABCdef *ghi* **jkl** 36pt.

The quick brown fox jumps. 14pt.

Round the rocks the ragged rascal ran. 6pt.

Ae 12 **A3** 72pt.

ABCdef *ghi* **jkl** 36pt.

The quick brown fox jumps. 14pt.

Round the rocks the ragged rascal ran. 6pt.

Figure 7.1. A sample of PostScript Century Old Style and Franklin Gothic Heavy typesetting output through (top) a laser printer at 300 dots per inch (dpi) and (bottom) through an imagesetter at 1700 dpi.

Hardware and Software

You need a relatively sophisticated computer system in order to use DTP most effectively. There are two types of computer system in common use which can run professional quality programs. These are the Apple and IBM Personal Computer systems. (The latter is usually abbreviated to PC. Computers compatible with the IBM Personal Computer are made by a wide range of manufacturers, all usually known by the generic name PC.)

You also need a 'mouse' which converts the movements of your hand on your desk onto the screen.

Almost as expensive as your computer will be your printer. To get good results you need a laser printer – and even that only gives you results comparable with a high-quality photocopier. And the best results can only be achieved if your laser printer can handle the page description language, PostScript.

PostScript is the computer software which enables your computer and printer to manipulate sophisticated images, such as typefaces and graphics, on the screen and print them. And PostScript capability for your printer obviously makes it more expensive!

PostScript is widely regarded as the industry 'standard' and hundreds of typefaces are now available in PostScript versions. You may come across other high-quality type formats which are now being developed for DTP, such as TrueType, but these are generally compatible with PostScript.

The most widely used PostScript DTP programs are Aldus PageMaker and Quark Xpress. Others are Ventura and DesignStudio. The software for each costs upwards of £500, but one of these is necessary if you want to do professional-quality work.

Producing Material on DTP

Text that is to be laid out on a DTP system can either be typed straight into the computer program or 'imported' from text produced in a word-processing or other program. Most common DTP programs can now import text from most common word-processing programs. Alternatively, the text may need to be first converted into a special format known as ASCII. ASCII stands for American Standard Codes for Information Interchange and is a format in which all the specialist codes that the typist may have introduced, such as underlines, tabulation, etc. have been removed. Your computer manual will explain how to convert text into ASCII format.

If you have an Optical Character Recognition (OCR) scanner you may be able to import any typed or printed text into your DTP system simply by passing it through. This process recognises the shapes of letters and converts them directly into text on the computer without the necessity of retyping. Any copy produced this way will still need to be checked carefully: the OCR process can only read clear, unbroken characters and unannotated text.

Matter that is being typed from scratch has to be typed carefully, particularly with regard to things like dashes, indents and space after punctuation. (It is at this stage that people begin to realise why typesetting is a craft which used to demand a long apprenticeship!)

With the text all in the computer, it is then a relatively simple matter to run through it and turn it into the typefaces, sizes and measures you require. Most DTP systems enable you to set up a grid on the screen, and fit your text and illustrations into it. You can also use this to ensure that, for instance, captions, headlines, subheads and folios are all set in the correct style from page to page.

The beauty of the more sophisticated DTP systems is that you actually see immediately what the result is of any decision you have taken. So if you want to produce a 16pp pamphlet, and you discover that setting it in 12pt type means that it comes out to 18pp, you can either cut some of the copy or change the typesize, measure, or number of lines per page. And if you don't like the typeface you can change it.

Illustrations

There are two basic ways of creating illustrative material on a DTP system. A scanner can be used to produce a digitised version of any existing image – either line or halftone. This uses up a lot of computer memory and does not always give as good results as a traditionally scanned or screened picture pasted onto the artwork by conventional means. Alternatively, graphics software can be used to 'draw' an image on screen, using the mouse. Tones and other effects can then be added by the computer. Images can then be stored, and manipulated in various ways. They can be expanded or condensed, enlarged or reduced. Again, this should all be explained in the software manual. If you cannot get as good results as you need from your software, you can of course insert boxes or a rough tracing using a mouse on the computer screen to represent where your illustrations go, and alter them as you please to fit your design. When you have finally decided the size, then you screen or scan it in the conventional manner. (See p.117 for how this is done.)

Special Design Effects

The manufacturers of some DTP programs have seen fit to introduce a number of effects which are very easy to incorporate into your design. Some of these are useful, but one of the temptations which inexperienced users frequently fall into is to use most if not all of them at once. For instance, some programs have the facility to turn any type into a shadow effect. This may have some display applications – but it often just looks out of place. See Figure 7.2, p.130.

Direct Entry Typing

There is a halfway house to implementing a complete DTP system which may be attractive to anyone producing books or pamphlets or other items with substantial amounts of text. This is to use a word processor to produce text which can be 'read' by an imagesetter.

The quick brown fox
The quick <u>brown</u> fox
The quick brown fox
The quick brown fox

Figure 7.2. Some of the typeface enhancements available in a DTP program. Use of them all at the same time is not usually recommended.

The output from most common word-processing programs – or text in ASCII format – can be used in this way, but obviously you need to check with your typesetters that they are willing and able to convert your material.

The typesetters will then add various 'tags' to determine size, style, measure, etc. Alternatively, you can input your own tags, usually between angle brackets, < >, at the relevant places in the text. This will save more money still.

The government's publishers, HMSO, and other big publishers use a British Standard Series of codes, Standard Generalised Markup Language (SGML). Other codes also exist and you may need to make further enquiries before getting too involved in this subject.

Sources
Useful introductions to DTP can be found in Susan Quilliam and Ian Grove-Stephensen, *Into Print* (London, BBC Books, 1990) and John Coops, *Teach Yourself Desktop Publishing* (Sevenoaks, Hodder and Stoughton, 1991). Kirty Wilson-Davies, Joseph St. John Bate and Michael Bernard, *Desktop Publishing*, 4th edition revised by Ron Strutt (London, Blueprint, 1991) is more advanced.

8

Printing and Paper

This chapter describes the main printing processes used today for the production of books and pamphlets and goes through what you need to do to get your material from final artwork into its finished form. Because it is most likely that your book will be produced by offset litho, the details mainly apply to that process. The chapter begins with a look at the different ways in which printing is carried out.

Letterpress

The first printing machines took multiple impressions from repeated inkings of a raised surface made up of type and illustration blocks. This simple process, called letterpress because it literally involves pressing type into paper, was the dominant method of printing for most of the last 500 years. It has only recently been superseded in volume by offset lithography. Letterpress is still widely used for the printing of paperback books (using a special 'belt' press), some newspapers and for packaging and cartons (using a variety of the letterpress method called flexography).

In traditional letterpress printing, the type, set in metal, is combined with illustration material etched photographically onto metal blocks, and locked together in a metal frame called a chase. The surface is inked by rollers and then prints directly onto the paper. The type and blocks are therefore mirror images of the final result.

The high-speed letterpress process used nowadays in some newspaper and paperback book printing rarely utilises traditional metal type. Type is usually set and made up into artwork in the same way as for litho. The artwork is then photographed to make a polymer or metal plate which has a raised surface.

The main advantages of traditional letterpress are that it is possible to achieve a very high quality of impression and a beautiful density of ink. It is still used by private press printers for limited editions for these reasons.

Lithography

Lithography (usually abbreviated to 'litho') as a process is almost 200 years old. It was first used for the printing of illustrations, but in the

131

latter part of the twentieth century it has been developed for the printing of just about everything. The process involves taking an impression from a flat surface, which is why it is called planographic. Lithography is based on the principle that oil and water do not mix. A printing plate is made and during the printing process the non-printing areas are coated with water so that the printing areas will receive the oil-based ink.

The modern litho process is, in fact, an 'offset' process. This means that the image from the printing plate is actually first transferred (or 'offset') onto a rubber surface, called a 'blanket'. The blanket is first dampened with water, then inked and finally pressed against the paper to transfer the image. Because the image is transferred twice, the original litho plate is the right way round rather than a mirror image. The press acts rather like a mangle, with the three cylinders for the plate, the blanket and the cylinder that presses the paper against the blanket pressing together. A rubber blanket is used because it protects the delicate surface of the printing plate from contact with the abrasive surface of the paper. Furthermore, water does not need to come into contact with the paper.

Unlike letterpress, the litho image is produced on one piece of metal photographically from artwork that combines text and illustrations. It is quicker to get a litho plate ready to print compared with the combination of type and blocks in letterpress printing. The process of getting any printing machine ready (by adjusting the ink and the paper feed etc.) is called 'make ready'.

The litho machine comes in many sizes. The smallest are designed mainly for in-house printing and can be operated without a high level of skill. They are often little more sophisticated than a stencil duplicator and use cheap plastic plates. Most general and commercial printers use medium-size 'sheet-fed' presses, which can print paper up to A2 (or sometimes A1) in size. A press is described as sheet-fed if the paper is fed into it in single sheets, whereas a press in which the paper is fed in on a reel is described as 'web-fed'. A web machine usually has folding and binding facilities also, so that the job emerges in a finished or near-finished state and it can run at speeds of up to 50,000 impressions per hour.

The medium-size sheet-fed press requires a skilled operator and is capable of running at quite fast speeds, up to 12,000 sheets per hour. Some can print more than one colour at a time. Some can print on both sides of the paper in one 'pass' through the machine (this is called 'perfecting'). A job that is to be printed in full colour is printed by overlaying the four constituent colours (yellow, magenta, cyan and black). A fuller description of four-colour printing is given on p.138.

Other Printing Processes

Gravure

In terms of volume, gravure is the second most commonly used printing process. Its use, however, is mainly confined to long-run magazine and catalogue work. A gravure plate is made photographically from artwork, and is prepared in much the same way as for litho. The surface of the plate is slightly indented. The inking process fills the indentations with ink and the paper is carried through the machine on a rubber-covered cylinder which presses it into the recesses of the plate. Gravure presses are generally very large and operate at very high speeds indeed (up to 50,000 impressions per hour). They can print on cheaper, thinner paper than can litho presses, which is why they are so attractive to publishers producing long runs of large magazines and catalogues.

Silk Screen

This process is commonly used to print very dense images, often on difficult surfaces like cloth. The process involves making a stencil, either by hand or photographically, and placing it on a fine mesh screen. Ink is forced through the image areas on the screen onto the paper. Automatic silk-screen presses can run at quite reasonable speeds – 6,000 impressions per hour – and are widely used for printing billboard posters and packaging. It can be a useful process for the small publisher, for instance for strong colours on book covers, since it is possible to get a more dense effect than with litho.

Xerography

This process is familiar as the method by which a photocopier operates. A combination of lenses and mirrors projects a reversed copy of the image on the glass onto a positively charged selenium drum or belt. This is dusted with negatively charged powder, which then sticks to the areas where no light has fallen, that is the image areas. The drum or belt then prints the image onto plain paper and the toner is fused to the paper by a heating element.

The quality of xerography has improved dramatically over the last few years and most so-called 'instant printing' is done on heavy-duty machines, which can often print on both sides of the sheet, and also collate and staple them. For small runs (say under 500 copies) this process is likely to be cheaper than printing. A disadvantage is that most high-speed machines only copy onto A4 paper, although A3 is becoming more common. Thus it is difficult to produce something that is designed to be folded down to A4 and bound with staples in the spine, since this has to be copied on A3 paper. But it is possible to use alternative methods of binding single A4 sheets, such as comb or wire binding.

It may even be possible to use 'perfect' binding if the publication is a reasonable length (usually at least 30 double-sided pages). For more about binding methods see pp.141–4.

These disadvantages do not apply if you are wanting to produce A5 format material. You may well find that it is cheaper to produce a short-run A5 pamphlet by copying than by any other method.

Laser Printing and Ink-jet Printing

Volume laser printing is making extremely rapid progress. Its use is mainly confined at present to the direct output from typesetting and desktop publishing systems, but it is becoming more widespread.

The image is created by a powder deposited on the paper by a process similar to xerography. But instead of being produced by a combination of lenses and mirrors the image is produced by a laser beam, controlled by a computer.

Ink-jet printing is similarly controlled by a computer. The image is produced by depositing tiny drops of ink on paper.

The major advantages these systems have are speed and flexibility. A book which is updated regularly can be held on computer and individual copies can be printed as and when needed. The quality of course is not as high as that of litho, and colour work is not yet possible. Laser printers cannot yet print out in very large sheet sizes, so conventional folding and binding methods are not usually used. The output is usually perfect bound or comb bound. (See pp. 141–4 for more about binding methods.) However, there is no doubt that this technology will become more and more important in years to come.

Paper

Most commercial publishers buy paper themselves, which they deliver directly to their printers. Generally, small publishers are better advised not to do the same. Your printers are already likely to buy paper regularly, in quite big quantities, and will know where they can get anything you are likely to require. They also know how many spare sheets to allow for making ready and for wastage. You should discuss with them what type and weight of paper you want and leave to them details such as the quantity and size of sheets they will require.

How Paper is Made

Most paper is made from liquid pulp on giant pressing, drying and rolling machines. These produce reels up to 7 metres wide at speeds of about 1,000 metres per hour. These reels can be then further treated before either being made into smaller reels suitable for a web press, or being cut into sheets for sheet-fed printing.

Types of Paper

Various kinds of paper and board (which is what printers usually call cover material and card) are available and some of those you may come across are listed below.

Newsprint is the cheap light paper used for printing newspapers. It is usually only available on reels and so can only be printed on a web (reel-fed) press.

Bond paper is a general printing paper, similar to that used for copying or stationery. It has a slightly rough finish and usually comes in weights of between 70 and 100 gsm (see below).

Cartridge paper is the term used for a heavier, slightly rough paper. It is often used for printing of books with no illustrations.

Art paper is coated with china clay and 'calendered' by rolling it between polished steel rollers. Matt art paper is also calendered but with less pressure so that the surface is consolidated by the process. Both are widely used for printing material which is heavily illustrated.

Blade coated cartridge (often just called coated cartridge) is midway between an uncoated and a matt art paper. It is perhaps the paper most widely used for general printing of material which is a mixture of type and illustrations, as it has enough surface to reproduce halftones well.

Chromo paper is coated on one side only and is used for posters, book jackets and labels.

Cast coated papers and boards have a very high gloss and are used for expensive packaging and cover material.

Specifying Paper Weight

The system used in the UK and most of Europe for expressing paper's weight is to specify the weight in grams of a single sheet of one square metre in area (grams per square metre, usually abbreviated to gsm).

Most general printing papers are in the range 80–175 gsm. Above this weight paper is too heavy for easy multiple folding. Board is usually in the weight range 225–300 gsm, if it is for general printing. Heavier boards, for instance for the covers of books or pamphlets, are usually in the range 300–450 gsm. Boards are sometimes specified in terms of their thickness in microns, rather than their weight in gsm.

For a book with no illustrations a medium-weight cartridge, in the range 90–135 gsm, is likely to be suitable. For a book with halftone illustrations, either a blade coated cartridge or a matt art paper is more suitable, again in the range 90–135 gsm. Cheap leaflets for handouts are usually printed on an 80 or 90 gsm bond, while brochures and more impressive leaflets are usually printed on slightly heavier paper, often 135 to 175 gsm coated cartridge, art or matt art.

What the Printers Do with Your Job

If your job is being printed by the offset litho process, the first thing that the printers will do with it is to convert all the artwork into negative photographic film. This is done by photographing it on a large camera, similar to the process camera used to make PMT prints (see p. 121). This negative film is then retouched with opaque fluid to ensure that the dark areas are completely impervious to light and then placed against a metal plate with a pre-sensitised surface and exposed to light, using a vacuum to ensure good contact. The metal plate is then developed and washed. The image area is now ready to attract water and repel ink and so the plate can be put onto the machine and used for printing.

That is the offset litho process in summary. We will now go through what happens in a little more detail and some further terms will be defined on the way.

Imposition

The organisation of the individual pages of a printed sheet so that they appear in the correct order when they are cut, folded and trimmed is called imposition. Artwork is usually made up as 'spreads', so that the designer can see the pages in the way they will appear in the final version. The printers need to reorganise these to suit the size of both the printing and folding machines, and this is usually done before the artwork is made into negative film.

There are various imposition arrangements, and the exact details of these need not concern us greatly. However it is important to know how many pages the printers will print in each section, since it will make quite a difference to the cost if they have to print another 16-page sheet just because the job is two pages longer than a multiple of 16. The size of each section is usually expressed as being, for instance, a 16-page sheet, 8 pages 'to view' – that is, with 8 pages on each side.

Another occasion on which you will need to know the imposition is if you are planning to use colour – either as a second 'spot' colour or, indeed, full colour – in just part of the book. If you can confine all the colour printing to just part of the printing run then it will save a lot on the cost. It is quite common, for instance, for colour to be used on just one side of the sheet only. This has the effect that every alternate spread can be printed in colour – so it is important that you, or your designer, is aware of this when laying out the illustrations.

Colour Separation

If your job is to be printed in more than one colour then the colours have to be separated before the negatives are made. This can be done in a number of ways. If the artwork has been provided already separated, then it is a simple matter to make up two (or more) separate sets of imposed negatives. Register marks are used to ensure that the images fit together exactly when the plates are printed onto the paper.

Alternatively, a 'mask' may be made which will ensure that only the parts of the artwork designed to print in the particular colour are exposed to light in the camera.

Finally, it is possible that you, or the designer, will not have provided artwork for a colour area, but simply have asked for, say, a boxed area to be filled with a colour. The printers' platemaker will do this directly onto the negative film, by painting in the area with opaque fluid.

Most DTP programs have the facility to provide colour-separated output. The use of professional-quality DTP programs to do even more of the pre-press work traditionally done by the platemaker is also becoming more widespread. It is now quite common for designers and production staff in commercial publishing to send completely separated four-colour film directly to printers.

Tints, Reversals and Other Special Effects

When an area is designed to be filled in with a tint a separate piece of film is prepared, by using a screen to give the effect of a tint. This negative is joined up – or 'stripped in' – to the main negative.

Reversals – when type or artwork is designed to appear as white on a solid black background – are also done as separate pieces of film and stripped in. They are simply made by making a positive piece of film rather than a negative, which will then of course reverse when the plate is made.

Halftone Illustrations

The negative film for halftone illustrations is also stripped into the main negative. The halftones are prepared by rephotographing the originals through a screen, at the same time enlarging or reducing them to the desired size. The effect is to convert a continuous tone original into a pattern of dots of different sizes, corresponding to the changes in density of the tones in the original. This can be seen in Figure 6.8, p.118.

Retouching the Negatives

Each piece of negative film is placed on a lightbox and examined carefully to ensure that the non-printing areas are completely opaque to light. Any specks of dust or marks on the artwork will show as spots of light on the lightbox and these are painted out with opaque fluid. Large areas to be made opaque are sometimes covered with a red film called 'rubylith', which is impermeable to light. This is also used to make masks for special effects such as dropping one coloured area into another.

Some printers impose the pages as pieces of negative film rather than as artwork. Whether or not they do this depends on technical details such as the size of their camera.

It is possible to have one final set of proofs made from the negatives before the plates are made. This is done by shining light through the negative onto a light-sensitive paper called a 'blue', or by its trade name, 'Ozalid'. These can then be checked to make sure that all illustrations etc. are in place and that any special effects such as tints and reversals have been done correctly.

Platemaking

Litho plates are fairly sensitive items and can deteriorate or get damaged in storage. The negatives are therefore the most vital thing for the printer to keep, since it is quite easy to make a new set of plates.

A plate is made by exposing its pre-sensitised surface to light through the negative. It is aligned precisely in a vacuum frame using holes punched on its edges and the edges of the negative. It is developed and washed after exposing.

It is possible to take proofs from the plates to be used for the job, either on a special proofing press or on the machine your job is going to be run on. This will be expensive and is not to be recommended unless you are absolutely convinced it is necessary.

However, you will probably want to see a colour proof if you are going to use full colour. This is usually done directly from the separated colour negatives, and is explained in the next section.

Full-colour Printing

There are three 'additive' primary colours, green, blue and red, from which all other colours are derived. White is produced when all three are combined in equal quantities. When one of the additive primaries is removed, the other two combined produce a separate colour. Red and blue produce magenta, green and blue produce cyan, red and green produce yellow. These three are therefore known as the 'subtractive' primaries. This piece of elementary physics is the basis for all colour printing.

The colour-printing process photographically separates all coloured originals into variegated images made up of these three subtractive primaries, plus black. Then, when the separated images are printed in their respective coloured inks, the colours come together again. This is therefore generally known as four-colour printing.

To separate the colours four separate filters are used, each corresponding to the respective additive primary colour, to make four negatives of the respective subtractive primary colour. Thus, a blue filter is used to absorb all light from the yellow components of the original, with the result that yellow is not recorded, giving the yellow negative. A green filter gives the negative for magenta and a red filter the negative for cyan. To get the black negative, either all three filters are used or no filters at all.

For illustrations, the light is shone through a screen as well as through the relevant filter, so that the negatives are in fact halftone dots. These correspond, as do black and white halftones, to the changes in colour and density across the whole of the illustration. The best results are achieved from transparencies but it is also possible to use a colour original.

The whole process of making a set of four-colour plates is highly automated and generally uses a piece of equipment called a scanner. Most small- and medium-sized printers actually use outside repro- duction houses who specialise in this kind of work.

Four-colour work is usually proofed before it is printed, either on a proofing press or by using an electrostatic proof called a 'Cromalin'. The proofs are supplied as a set showing the full effect of all four colours printed together and as a series of 'progressives', showing the effect as each colour is overlaid on the one before. This makes it easier for you to correct the overall colour, by increasing or reducing the quantities of the constituent colours.

It is not possible to go into more detail about four-colour printing in this book, not least because it is only printed in black! Furthermore, the budgets of most small publishers do not run to the expense of this process. Colour is a specialised area and you are advised to acquire more detailed knowledge if you are going to embark on it regularly. Some books on the subject are listed in the Further Reading section, pp.150–3.

Machining

The publisher does not need to know much more about printing machines themselves, apart from the size of paper they print on and the speed at which they operate. Modern machines are highly automated with sophisticated controls for inking and maintaining register between the colours.

However, there is nothing to beat a visit while your job is being printed, to experience the smell of wet ink on paper. Printers are rightly proud of their craft and are usually pleased to meet their customers. And when you see a printing press in action you get a real feel for what remains a slightly magical process, that turns mere words scribbled on scraps of paper into that most permanent piece of ephemera, a book.

Sources
David Bann, *The Print Production Handbook* (London, Macdonald, 1986)
is probably the most useful recent book on methods of printing and
paper. Hugh Williamson, *Methods of Book Design,* 3rd edition (London,
Yale University Press, 1983) also contains relevant material. Both books
have useful glossaries.

9

Finishing and Binding

The term 'finishing' is used in the printing industry to describe all those processes which go on after a job is printed to make up the final product. These range from folding and collating to the addition of special protection such as lamination. Binding is the term used to describe all the different ways of attaching covers to the pages of a magazine, pamphlet or book.

Folding and Cutting

Nearly all jobs are folded and/or cut. The only exception is when a job is printed on single sheets of paper which are already the right size when they go through the press.

The printers will have made allowances for how a job will be folded and cut when it is being imposed. For instance, if a simple A4 leaflet is being printed on a machine with a capacity for A3 or bigger, then it will probably have been imposed to print as a 'work and turn'. This means that only one set of negatives and plates needs to be made, since once the paper has been printed on one side it merely needs to be turned over and printed again from the same plate on the reverse.

More complicated impositions may need to be cut on the guillotine before they are folded.

Guillotines and folding machines are often very sophisticated pieces of precision equipment with computer-controlled settings so that precisely the same cut or fold is repeated throughout the run.

A guillotine is also used to trim all the rough edges off a job after it is printed.

Binding Methods

There are two methods of binding which the small publisher is likely to use. The first is the insertion of wire staples into the spine, called wire saddle stitching. The second is the glueing of individual leaves into a cover, called perfect binding. These are described in turn below. Some other methods of binding are also described.

Saddle Stitching and Stab Stitching

Wire saddle stitching is the simplest form of binding. It is also possible to bind a publication using thread stitching in the spine, which is called thread saddle stitching. With both of these methods all the folded sheets which make up a complete job are collated, combined with the cover and positioned on a saddle under a head that inserts wire staples (cut from a continuous roll of wire) or thread.

If there is no separate cover added during the collating process and the cover matter is printed on the front and back pages of the job then this is called a 'self cover'. This is useful for thin pamphlets and magazines since the printers do not have to use heavier and more expensive cover material. Poor-quality text paper, however, may not stand up to much wear and tear if it is used for a cover, so this may not be an attractive option.

A variant of saddle stitching uses staples punched into the side of the publication about 6mm from the spine. This is called side stitching or stab stitching and is often used on heavy magazines before a cover is glued on.

Saddle stitching cannot be used for very thick publications. The maximum number of pages that can be bound in this way varies according to the thickness of the paper being used but is normally somewhere between 80 and 100. If your publication is longer then you will need to use another method of binding.

Perfect Binding

Perfect binding is a method of glueing individual pages inside a cover. During the process, the individual sheets are folded into sections, which are then collated, or 'gathered', together. The gathered sections have about 3mm trimmed off the back fold (which means the pages are now individual leaves) and the cut spine is then roughened by a grinder. This 'block' of leaves is then glued at the spine and has the cover material pressed onto it. On fast, fully automated perfect-binding lines the binder is usually combined with a guillotine which then cuts the head, tail and foredge to give a flush finish.

Perfect binding can be used to bind individual pages produced by, for instance, a photocopier. This can be an attractive way of binding a simply produced report.

Perfect binding can only be used on publications above a length of about 48 pages. One of its main advantages, of course, is that it provides a spine on which the title can be printed, so that it can be seen when placed on a shelf. If you are planning to sell your publication in bookshops it is almost a necessity for it to have a spine.

Sewn Binding

It is possible to give extra strength to a paperback book by sewing it. With this method each section of the book is sewn through its spine and then the spines of all the sections are joined together using more thread. The cover is then glued to the spine and trimmed on three edges, in a similar process to perfect binding.

This process is worth considering if you are producing a heavy book, or one which you want people to keep for some time. It is difficult to break the spine or pull out the pages of a sewn book, so it has a degree of permanence. It is also considerably cheaper than 'cased' (hardback) binding, which is described next.

Cased (Hardback) Binding

The hardback binding of books is now almost completely automated. A gathered set of pages either has endpapers made of strong paper glued to its front and back, or the first and last page of the book are used as endpapers. They should, of course, in this case not be printed on either the first and last page. (The book is then described as 'self-endpapered'.)

The gathered and endpapered sections are sewn and trimmed. The spine is 'lined' by glueing a strip of rough paper or cloth to reinforce the joint. The spine can then be 'rounded and backed' (shaped to make it convex), or left square. The book block is then 'cased in', with glue being attached to the cover material and the complete book pressed flat.

The cover material or 'case' is made by wrapping and glueing cloth or imitation cloth around three pieces of board for front, spine and back. The cloth can be plain or printed.

A process called blocking is used to stamp the title and any other material onto the case, often using a metal foil such as imitation gold. The dies used to stamp the cases are either 'brasses' or cheaper alternatives called 'Chemacs'.

A cased book usually has a paper jacket wrapped around it. This is often similar to the cover of any paperback version but, because the dimensions of a cased book are different, it has to be printed in a separate operation.

Dummies

If you are going to the expense of cased binding then you may find it advisable to get the binder to make up a 'dummy'. This is a sample of the book, using the correct number of pages of the paper for the book, bound in the correct material. You, or your designer, can use this to ensure that you have the correct spine width and enough flap material for the jacket.

Spiral, Wire Comb and Plastic Comb Binding

All these methods are used to produce reports and manuals where the ability to lie flat is important. The machinery is often very cheap and readily available in instant print shops. Each method involves punching (or 'drilling') a set of holes through a set of collated sheets and covers and inserting a wire coil (spiral), a wire comb often called by its trade name (Wiro) or plastic comb.

A type of binding known as 'Full Canadian' or 'Half Canadian' allows cover material to be wrapped around a wire comb, thus creating a spine on which the title can be printed.

Varnishing and Laminating

Either of these two processes can be used to give a high gloss to the cover material and to protect it from finger marks and other dirt. Varnishing involves coating the cover with a special varnish (sometimes drying it under ultraviolet light). Laminating applies a very thin film of glossy plastic to the whole cover. Both methods are readily available and either is well worth the few extra pence it adds to the unit cost of each job to prevent your expensive production looking shabby after a few weeks on the bookshop shelf.

Sources

David Bann, *The Print Production Handbook* (London, Macdonald, 1986) contains useful material on methods of finishing and binding, as does Hugh Williamson, *Methods of Book Design,* 3rd edition (London, Yale University Press, 1983). Both books have useful glossaries.

Checklists

Commissioning Author

- Discuss scope, audience, format, illustrations, etc.
- Send house style, typing guidelines, references guidelines.
- If using author's disk, check compatibility.

When Typescript/Disks Arrive

- Check that typescript is complete.
- Check that printed copy is the same as that on disk.
- Check that any commands, etc., that the author has inserted for direct entry typing are correct.
- Cast off and determine final extent.
- Estimate production costs.
- Check copyright clearance of quotations and illustrations.

Copy-editing

Text
- Mark new pages and, if necessary, any (e.g. contents page) that should be new rectos.
- Mark on first page of text whether numbering should start as p.1, p.3, or something else.
- Draw up style sheet.
- If author has used numbered paragraphs or sections, ascertain whether this is necessary. Remove if not.
- Impose house style on abbreviations, capitalisation, dates and time, italic and roman, -ise/-ize endings, numbers, etc.
- Check cross-references, but leave typescript page numbers legible for ease of reference later.
- Mark approximate position for figurative material and change references to 'the following table', etc.
- Code subheadings – are there too many levels?
- Check indentation on lists and quoted matter.
- Make numbering systems in lists consistent.
- Note any major changes to text needed to discuss with author.

145

- Note any problems for designer, e.g. special typefaces or symbols, etc.
- Check that reference indicators are all present.
- Watch out for stereotypes and other unconscious discrimination in language.
- Supply instructions for headlines.

Prelims
- Check all copy is complete, and write out copy if not.
- Mark each section with the folio number it will begin on.
- Check other books in series/author's other books, if used.
- Check title, subtitle, author(s) name(s) are same as copy for jacket.
- Check copyright notice.
- Supply publication history, publisher and printer's name and address, CIP data line, ISBN (for both editions if separate paper and cased).
- Check contents list against text.
- Check level of contents entries – do all levels of subheadings need to be included?
- Check lists of illustrations, tables, other figurative matter against matter provided.

References
- Is author's system consistent and adequate?
- Remove unnecessary Latinisms – op. cit., loc. cit. and so on.

End Matter
- Mark up appendices as fresh pages if necessary.
- Check style in bibliography, and chase author for missing details.
- If no glossary, is one needed?
- Check list of addresses and telephone numbers – are they up to date? Spot check a few to be sure.

Jacket/Cover Copy
- Check same as title page.
- Check for completeness – ISBN, bar code, price (if used).
- Check that any variations for paper/cased editions are marked.

Design
- Devise styles for all parts of the book before beginning typesetting.
- Check all chapter titles are much the same length – base style on the longest.
- Devise style for all levels of subheadings – if too many, try to negotiate change with editor/author.
- Ensure artists know how to produce camera-ready artwork.
- Check reproducibility of all illustrations, and ensure that they will reproduce at the size they will appear.

- Mark up reduction/enlargement on an overlay or photocopy for each illustration.
- Number each illustration, and also mark with folio number.

After Typesetting

Proofs
- Check galley/first proofs against copy, or arrange for someone else to do so.
- Collate all author's corrections onto master set of proofs, and colour code (typesetter's errors in red; author changes in blue) to avoid being overcharged.
- If possible, provide cross-references, etc. from a rough paste-up of galley/first proofs so that as many corrections as possible are all done at the same time.
- Check any designer's rough paste-up before it goes to typesetters with corrected galleys.
- Provide indexer with a copy of page proofs as quickly as possible so that this does not delay production.
- Check all captions to figurative matter.
- Cross-check contents and other lists with page proofs.
- Check folio numbering, and correct placement of verso and recto pages.
- Recheck all pages on page proofs, not just earlier corrections from galleys.
- Check jacket/cover proof and artwork.

Printing
- Check Ozalid to ensure colour separations, tints, etc. are correct.
- Check colour proof for quality of colour printing.

Binding
- Check final spine width before cover printing, and adjust jacket/cover artwork if necessary.

Finally
- Examine finished book carefully, and complain promptly if something is wrong.
- Calculate actual cost, and degree of error in estimate.
- Keep a copy on file with any mistakes marked, for correction if a reprint is needed.
- Get artwork, etc. back from printer. (It is your property. Films and plates are printer's.)
- Return any illustrations, etc. on loan promptly to avoid excess hire fees.

Useful Organisations

This list is essentially of addresses relevant to this book. Inclusion in this list does not imply any form of recommendation.

Arts Council of Great Britain, 14 Great Peter Street, London SW1P 3NQ. Tel: 071 333 0100. Fax: 071 973 6590.
ASLIB, Association for Information Management, Information House, 26–27 Boswell Street, London WC1N 3JZ. Tel: 071 430 2671.
Association of Illustrators, 1 Colville Place, London W1P 1HN Tel: 071 636 4100.
Association of Learned and Professional Society Publishers, Professor Bernard Donovan, 48 Kelsey Lane, Beckenham, Kent BR3 3NE. Tel: 081 658 0459.
Association of Little Presses, 89a Petherton Road, London N5 2QT. Tel: 071 226 2657.
Book Trust, Book House, 45 East Hill, London SW18 2QZ. Tel: 081 870 9055. Fax: 081 874 4790.
Book Trust Scotland, 15a Lynedoch Street, Glasgow G3 6EF. Tel: 041 332 0391. Fax: 041 331 2645.
Booksellers Association of Great Britain and Ireland, 272–274 Vauxhall Bridge Road, London SW1V 1BA. Tel: 071 834 5477. Fax: 071 834 8812.
British Copyright Council, Copyright House, 29–33 Berners Street, London W1P 4AA. Tel: 071 580 5544.
British Library National Bibliographic Services, Boston Spa, Wetherby, West Yorks LS23 7BQ. Tel: 0937 546612.
Congor Llyfrau Cymraeg/Welsh Books Council, Castell Brychan, Aberystwyth, Dyfed SY23 2JB. Tel: 0970 624151.
Independent Publishers Guild, 25 Cambridge Road, Hampton, Middlesex TW12 2JL. Tel: 081 979 0250.
International Publishers Association, 3 avenue de Miremont, 1206 Geneva, Switzerland. Tel: 010 41 22 46 30 18. Fax: 010 41 22 47 57 17.
Irish Book Publishers Association, Book House Ireland, 65 Middle Abbey Street, Dublin 1, Ireland. Tel: 010 353 1 730108. Fax: 010 353 1 730620.
KTP Ltd (bar code suppliers), PO Box 15, Beverley, Yorks HU17 8DY. Tel: 0482 867321. Fax: 0482 882712.

National Union of Journalists, Acorn House, 314 Grays Inn Road, London WC1X 8DP. Tel: 071 278 7916. Fax: 071 837 8143.
Publishers Association, 19 Bedford Square, London WC1B 3HJ. Tel: 071 580 6321/5. Fax: 071 636 5375.
Radical Bookseller, 265 Seven Sisters Road, London N4 2DE. Tel: 081 802 8773.
Scottish Publishers Association, The Scottish Book Centre, 137 Dundee Street, Edinburgh EH11 1BG. Tel: 031 228 6866. Fax: 031 228 4333.
Society of Freelance Editors and Proofreaders, c/o 16 Brenthouse Road, London E9 6QG. Tel; 081 986 4868.
Society of Indexers, c/o 38 Rochester Road, London NW1 9JJ. Tel: 071 916 7809.
Society of Young Publishers, 12 Dyott Street, London WC1A 1DF.
Standard Book Numbering Agency, 12 Dyott Street, London WC1A 1DF. Tel: 071 836 8911. Fax: 071 836 4342.
J Whitaker and Sons Ltd (publishers and services to publishing), 12 Dyott Street, London WC1A 1DF. Tel: 071 836 8911. Fax: 071 836 2909.
Women in Publishing, 12 Dyott Street, London WC1A 1DF. Tel: 071 836 8911. Fax: 071 836 2909.

Further Reading

This annotated reading list is not a true bibliography (see p.44). It is provided in this style to give general guidance both for reference and further reading. Most books mentioned below were in print when this book went to press – if not, they should still be available from libraries.

General Books on Publishing

General advice on most aspects of getting into print can be found in a number of books.

Jenny Vaughan, *Getting into Print* (London, Bedford Square Press, 1988) is a very useful short book. It covers developments in new technology and is full of solid practical advice.

Audrey and Philip Ward, *The Small Publisher: A Manual* (Cambridge, Oleander Press, 1979) covers most of the problems a small publisher will face.

This book's companion volume, Bill Godber, Robert Webb and Keith Smith, *Marketing for Small Publishers* (London, Journeyman Press, 1992) is a practical guide to marketing, promoting and distributing books once they are published.

Writing

The essential primer for people writing 'official' English has long been Gowers' *Plain Words*. Now in its third edition (Sir Ernest Gowers, *The Complete Plain Words*, 3rd edition revised by Sidney Greenbaum and Janet Whitcut (London, HMSO, 1986) and also a Penguin Guide) it is a manual full of wisdom and sense.

A book published by the Open University Course Team, *Plain English*, 2nd edition (Milton Keynes, Open University Press, 1982) is very helpful for anyone wanting a structured programme for writing in plain English.

The standard reference book, H.W. Fowler, *Modern English Usage*, 2nd edition revised by Sir Ernest Gowers (Oxford, Oxford University Press, 1965) remains a good reference for points of grammar, while G.V. Carey, *Mind the Stop*, revised edition (Harmondsworth, Penguin, 1976) is a concise guide to punctuation. Bill Bryson, *Penguin Dictionary of*

Troublesome Words, (London, Penguin, 1984) is useful both because it is arranged alphabetically and also because it acts as a succinct summary of contemporary thinking on many points of grammar and style.

There are a number of books on writing for newspapers. The plain, direct style advocated by two well-known journalists has much to be commended for general writing too. Harold Evans, *Newsman's English* (London, Heinemann, 1972) is the standard text for trainee journalists. Keith Waterhouse, *Waterhouse on Newspaper Style* (London, Viking, 1989) is a primer for tabloid newspaper writers, by one of the craft's current masters. In its own words, it is a 'polemic against shoddy or tired writing and a plea for fresh and workmanlike writing'. His later book, Keith Waterhouse, *English our English (and How to Sing It)* (London, Viking, 1991), is a manual for general writing.

John Whale, *Put it in Writing* (London, Dent, 1984) and John Fairfax and John Moat, *The Way to Write* (London, Elm Tree Books, 1981) both deal more with 'creative' writing.

Two books published by Penguin, Bruce M. Cooper, *Writing Technical Reports* (Harmondsworth, Penguin, 1964) and Doris Wheatley, *Report Writing* (Harmondsworth, Penguin, 1988) both cover how to set out and compose reports. Although the former is very dated, its essential advice remains sound.

Writing on Computers
The special skills needed by authors producing their own disks for typesetting and DTP have spawned a number of advice manuals. A comprehensive guide through the potential minefield is Jane Dorner, *Writing on Disk* (Hatfield, John Taylor Book Ventures, 1992).

Editing

Judith Butcher, *Copy-editing: The Cambridge Handbook,* 3rd edition (Cambridge, Cambridge University Press, 1992) is perhaps the most useful single purchase any aspiring small publisher could make. Not only is it the most thorough UK guide to copy-editing, it is also a model publisher's handbook with its plain commonsense approach and clarity of writing. The recently published third edition has been extensively revised to cover the problems of writing and editing material on disk.

The Chicago Manual of Style, 13th edition (Chicago, University of Chicago Press, 1982) is impressively comprehensive. *Hart's Rules for Compositors and Readers at the University Press, Oxford*, 39th edition (Oxford, Oxford University Press, 1983) is slim, but often helpful.

The Oxford Dictionary for Writers and Editors, 12th edition (Oxford, Oxford University Press, 1981) complements *Hart's Rules* and is a handy guide on points of style. Together, these two books make up

OUP's style guide – this may seem to some to be rather dated for today's use.

Besides the *Daily Mirror*'s house style guide, now published as *Waterhouse on Newspaper Style* (see above), a number of other newspapers and magazine style guides are available, such as those for *The Economist* and *The Times*. They all have points of interest for anyone compiling their own house style guide, not least because of the differences between them.

Equal Opportunities in Print

Casey Miller and Kate Swift, *The Handbook of Non-Sexist Writing for Writers, Editors and Speakers*, 2nd British edition (London, Women's Press, 1989) is a guide to non-sexist and anti-sexist writing.

The NUJ Book Branch has published a useful short pamphlet on the same subject. National Union of Journalists Book Branch, *Non-sexist Code of Practice for Book Publishing* (London, NUJ, 1982).

Very little seems to have been published as guidelines for anti-racist writing. A pamphlet, regrettably now out of print, from the Methodist Church, Ethnic Minorities in Methodism Working Group, *Check It* (London, Methodist Church Division of Social Responsibility, 1984), is useful, but of course concentrates on the church's own material. (Division of Social Responsibility, 1 Central Buildings, London SW1H 9NH.)

The London-based Disability Resource Team published a pack on good practice for local authorities in providing services and access for people with disabilities, *People with Disabilities: Models of Good Practice for Local Authorities* (London, LBDRT, 1987). This is now out of print but the useful section on publishing for people with disabilities, including suggestions on how and when to provide tape-recorded information, information in Braille and large print and translation into languages other than English, can be obtained from them at a fee. (DRT, Bedford House, 125 Camden High Street, London NW1 7JR.)

Design

The type manufacturer Linotype has published a very good introductory pamphlet on design, Linotype, *Pleasures of Design* (Cheltenham, Linotype, 1989).

Alex Brown, *In Print: Text and Type* (New York, Watson-Guptill, 1989) is a thorough and up-to-date American book on typography, design and book production in the era of desktop publishing.

John Laing (editor), *Do-it-yourself Graphic Design* (London, Ebury Press, 1984) is a practical, simple guide very useful for beginners, while Alan

Swann, *Basic Design and Layout* (Oxford, Phaidon, 1987) is helpful for someone with a little experience.

Ruari McLean, *The Thames and Hudson Manual of Typography* (London, Thames and Hudson, 1980) is a handbook full of sense from one of Britain's most respected postwar designers and writers. Douglas Martin, *An Outline of Book Design* (London, Blueprint/Publishers Association, 1989) marries the classic approach to the new technology. Oliver Simon, *Introduction to Typography,* 2nd edition, edited by David Bland (London, Faber and Faber, 1963) remains remarkably up to date, given its age.

Jonathan Zeitlyn, *Effective Publicity and Design* (London, Journeyman Press, 1992) is a handbook on simple design techniques, with many useful insights into the thought processes involved.

Desktop Publishing

Two books provide a useful introduction to DTP without overwhelming the reader with technical jargon. These are Susan Quilliam and Ian Grove-Stephensen, *Into Print* (London, BBC Books, 1990) and John Coops, *Teach Yourself Desktop Publishing* (Sevenoaks, Hodder and Stoughton, 1991). Kirty Wilson-Davies, Joseph St. John Bate and Michael Bernard, *Desktop Publishing,* 4th edition revised by Ron Strutt (London, Blueprint, 1991) is more technical but very useful.

Production

David Bann, *The Print Production Handbook* (London, Macdonald, 1986) is a useful handbook on many aspects of print production, including full-colour printing, with a very full glossary.

Hugh Williamson, *Methods of Book Design,* 3rd edition (London, Yale University Press, 1983) is more about production than design. It is comprehensive, but now rather shows its age.

Glossary

A0, A1, A2, etc. Series of finished, trimmed paper sizes devised by the International Organisation for Standardisation.

Ampersand Symbol for the abbreviation for 'and': &.

Appendix Subsidiary material for a book which is set out in the end matter.

Art paper Paper coated with thin layer of china clay used for printing jobs that contain halftone illustrations. Usually has a glossy finish – if it is matt it is called 'matt art'.

Artwork The complete original matter which is used for reproduction by the camera. Should not be marked except with a light-blue pencil.

Ascender Top part of a lower case letter stretching above the x-height, in d, h, f, etc.

Author's correction Corrections made to a proof by the author and/or the editor that alter the text from the original copy. Usually charged back to the publishers.

Back The margin between the spine and the printed image.

Bastard A non-standard format.

Bibliography List of books and other sources referred to or used in the preparation of a text.

Bleed Illustration or background colour, etc., which extends beyond the page edge.

Blob or bullet Solid circular or square symbol used for emphasis or in lists.

Blocking The process of stamping an impression from a die in foil, often used on covers. Can be used 'blind' to create a raised or depressed surface.

Blurb Description of the book and its contents used on the cover.

Bold Type with thickened strokes, a bolder version of another typeface.

Bond A medium-weight writing, typing or printing paper, usually in the range 70–100 gsm.

Bullet or blob Solid circular or square symbol used for emphasis or in lists.

Cataloguing in Publication data (CIP) A bibliographical description of a book, supplied by the national libraries such as British Library and US Library of Congress, to assist librarians in cataloguing it.

Camera ready copy (CRC) Another word for artwork.

Caps Abbreviation for capitals.

Cartridge A medium- to heavy-weight paper, with a slightly rough finish. Widely used in printing material that has text only.

Cased Bound in hard covers, by a process involving glueing endpapers both to the pages and the cover.

Cast coated High-gloss finish for paper or board.

Cast-off A calculation of amount of printed space that the copy will occupy when set in a given typeface and measure.

Chromo Paper coated on one side only, often used for printing posters, jackets and labels.

Coated cartridge (blade coated cartridge) Midway between an uncoated and matt art paper. Widely used in printing material that combines text and illustrations.

Cold composition Typesetting by any method other than hot metal.

Continuous tone see *Halftone.*

Copy Raw material, such as typescript.

Copyholder Person who assists a proofreader by reading out the text for the other to check.

Copyright The legal ownership of a piece of writing or an illustration.

Cromalin Proprietary name for a proofing system involving overlays of transparent film often used for checking multi-coloured work.

Crop Cutting down or masking an illustration or photograph.

Cross-head Subheading. (Technically a centred subheading.)

Cut lines The edges of the paper on which typesetting, etc. has been printed out, which show up as marks on a proof.

Dedication or epigraph A page in the preliminary matter devoted to a dedication or relevant quotation.

Descender Bottom part of a lower case letter, stretching below the x-height, in g, j, p, etc.

Desktop publishing A computer software program which allows text to be arranged in a variety of styles and sizes and combined with illustrations and graphics. Usually outputted to a laser printer held in house, and therefore allows the production of near artwork-quality material in a form ready for the printer.

Digitisation The process of converting a letterform or other image into a series of digital signals for storage on a computer.

Dot leaders A series of dots used to link two items, such as chapter titles to page numbers in a list of contents.

Dots per inch (dpi) Degree of resolution produced by laser printer or imagesetter.

Double-page spread (or just spread) A pair of pages which will face each other in the final printed form.

Drop Gap at the top of a page or column before the printed image starts.

Drop initial/cocked initial The first letter of a chapter or section of text, set in larger type and occupying space either on two or more of the following lines of text (drop) or above the first line of text (cocked). To accommodate this, the measure of the text setting has to be adjusted.

Dummy A sample book, with the same number of pages as the final book, using the paper and binding process that will be used in the final manufacture. Made to ensure that jackets, etc. are made to correct size.

Em The square of any size of type, i.e. a 10pt em is 10pts wide. The measure or width of any piece of typesetting is always expressed in 12pt ems, sometimes called picas.

Em rule Rule one em wide (—) used in typesetting to indicate the omission of a word or part of a word, or as a parenthetical dash.

En A measurement half the width of an em.

En rule Rule one en wide (–) used in typesetting as a parenthetical dash or to replace the word 'to'.

End matter The parts of a book which customarily appear after the text.

Endpaper The sheets of paper used at each end of a case-bound book to fasten the case to the first and last sections.

Extent The number of pages in a book or pamphlet.

Family A group of series of types from a single basic design, each with a variation in weight, width, italicisation or some other feature.

Figurative matter The parts of a book comprising tables, diagrams and other figures.

Figure An illustration printed in the text.

Folio (1) A single sheet of typescript; (2) a printed page number.

Footnote, endnote Reference or explanatory note that appears at the foot of a page (footnote) or at the end either of a chapter or of the whole text (endnote).

Foredge The margin between the printed image and the outside edge of the page.

Foreword, preface, introduction Foreword: introductory remarks about a book or its author, often written by someone else. Preface: personal note by the author, explaining how the book came to be written. Introduction: matter dealing wholly with the subject of the book.

Format The final trimmed page size of a book or pamphlet or the final folded size of a leaflet.

Fount The complete characters of one size of one typeface. The proof correction mark 'Wrong fount (w.f.)' is used to indicate that a letter of the wrong design or wrong size has been included. (Also font.)

Four-colour process The printing process whereby full-colour material is reproduced from the three subtractive primary colours: yellow, magenta and cyan, plus black.

Frontispiece Illustration facing the title page.

Full out Adjoining the margin. If a passage starts full out it is not indented.

Galley proofs Proofs taken from the typesetting machine as they are generated, i.e. in long strips.

Gathering Placing the printed sections in the right order before binding.

Glossary Alphabetical list of definitions of technical or foreign words, etc.

Grams per square metre (gsm) Paper weight, expressed as the weight of a single sheet of 1 square metre measured in grams.

Gravure A method of printing using plates with slight indentations in the surface. Often used for long-run magazines etc.

Grid (1) The arrangement of design elements in a repeating pattern throughout a book; (2) sheets with an outline preprinted in non-reproducing colour to facilitate accurate paste-up of artwork.

Half-title The first printed page of a book, preceding the frontispiece and title page.

Halftone The process by which various shades of grey are simulated by a pattern of black dots of various sizes. The continuous tone original (usually a photograph) is photographed again through a fine mesh screen which breaks the picture into dots.

Headline In a book, the headings set at the top of each page. Sometimes called *running heads*.

Hot-metal composition Generic term for mechanical methods of setting metal type, usually for letterpress printing.

House style A guide to spelling, punctuation, etc. used throughout a publishing house to ensure that all copy is treated consistently.

Hyphenation and justification program Computer program used in typesetting to give even left- and right-hand margins and which automatically decides wordbreaks in order to avoid gappy setting.

IBM Composer A sophisticated golf-ball typewriter which can set type in a variety of sizes and founts.

Identifier Marker in text, usually a typographic character such as an asterisk or a superior numeral, to identify the presence of a note.

Imagesetting Generic name for all types of typesetting where letters are assembled from digitised images held on a computer and printed out on light-sensitive paper or film.

Imposition The arrangement of pages by the printer so that they will appear in the right order and with the correct margins when the printed sheets are folded and trimmed.

Index Alphabetical list of subjects in a book, together with references to the pages on which they are covered.

International Standard Book Number (ISBN) Unique 10-digit number identifying every edition of every book.

Italic Sloping characters.

Justified setting Typesetting that has even left- and right-hand margins.

Kern The portion of a letter which overhangs the letter next to it.

Kerning The automatic adjustment of space between certain combinations of letters so that they overhang each other, to avoid unsightly spacing.

Key line Lines drawn by the designer on the artwork to show the position of illustrations, etc.

Laminating Process of covering or encapsulating an item in a thin transparent plastic film for protection.

Landscape Illustration or format where the width is greater than the height. The opposite is called 'portrait'.

Laser printing Process of printing an image through depositing a powder on a surface by an electrostatic process (similar to xerography), with the image being created by modulations in a laser beam.

Leading The spacing between lines of type.

Leaf Two pages which back onto each other.

Letraset A brand of dry transfer lettering.

Letterform The shape of an individual letter in a particular typeface.

Letterpress The process of printing from a raised surface.

Line drawing A drawing which consists of black lines only, with no greys. Grey areas are simulated using a tint or shading.

Literal A mistake made by the operator when setting type. Sometimes called *typos* – typographical errors.

Lower case Letters in their non-capital form.

Machining Printing. The printing machine operator is called a machine minder.

Make ready The adjustment necessary to the printing machine at the beginning of every job to ensure an even impression, correct position of the image, etc.

Make up The process of making pages from galleys of typeset material and illustrations, etc.

Mark up Instructions to typesetters covering each item in a typescript.

Marked set Proofs marked with corrections and queries raised by the typesetter's proofreader.

Mask Piece of card or film with cut-outs used in colour separation to ensure that only the relevant parts of a piece of artwork are exposed to light by the camera.

Measure The width to which a complete line of type is set.

Mechanical An American word for artwork.

Newsprint Cheap, lightweight paper with a coarse surface used for newspaper printing.

Offset lithography The process of printing whereby an image is transferred from a flat plate onto a rubber blanket and then onto paper.

Orphan see *Widow*.

Overmatter Typeset material which cannot fit into the space allocated to it, which needs to be cut at page proof stage.

Ozalid Proprietary name for the final proof taken from negative or positive film exposed to a specially coated paper which is then developed in ammonia. Also called blues, dyeline or diazo.

Parentheses, brackets, braces Correct names for ( ), [ ] and { } respectively.

Paste-up A paged layout showing all the type etc. in position. Sometimes used as a name for artwork.

Perfect binding Binding for a book with individual sheets glued into a cover.

Photomechanical transfer (PMT) A system for making very good quality prints for use in preparing artwork. Used to make illustrations the right size, preparing reverse outs and, when used in conjunction with a screen, for making halftone reproductions of photographs. See *Halftone, Reverse out*.

Pica A measurement of 12pts.

Pixels The individual components of an image on a visual display unit or in the output of an imagesetter.

Plate The (usually metal) image carrier used to transfer ink to blanket on a litho press.

Point (abbreviated to pt) A unit for measuring the size of type defined as 0.13837 inch (approximately 1/72 inch).

Prelims The parts of a book which customarily appear before the text.

Process camera Large rostrum camera used to make PMTs and negatives for litho platemaking.

Proof (1) Copy of typesetting for checking and correction; (2) copy of text and illustrations for checking and correction of size, colour balance, correct positioning of all elements, etc.

Range To align.

Recto Right-hand page.

Reduction The amount by which an illustration is to be photographically reduced before reproduction.

References Bibliographical details of books, etc., cited in the text.

Register The accurate superimposition of colours in multi-colour printing (helped by registration marks which are placed on the separate pieces of artwork to show their correct position).

Repro Artwork-quality typesetting.

Reverse out To reverse black to white in a particular area so that the final appearance is of white type, etc. on a black or coloured background.

Rough Designer's rough sketch.

Rubylith Film which is not permeable to light, used to make masks or to cover non-printing areas on the negative in platemaking.

Run on Continue on the same line, rather than starting a new paragraph or line.

Running heads see *Headlines*.

Saddle stitch A method of binding by inserting wire staples or thread in the spine.

Sans serif Type without serifs.

Scanning Electronic process whereby transparencies or other reproduction material are scanned by a light or laser beam to create halftones suitable for reproduction. Usually used in conjunction with colour separation for four-colour printing.

Screen A fine mesh grid, placed against light-sensitive negative film or PMT material through which light reflected from a continuous tone original is passed, so that it can be converted into a halftone.

Section The individual element of printed and folded paper which is gathered together with other sections to be bound into a book or pamphlet. (Also known as a *signature*.)

Self cover Pamphlet, etc. where the cover is printed on the front and back pages of the rest of the job and therefore does not need to be collated with a separately printed cover before binding.

Separated artwork Artwork that has been prepared as a series of overlays, one for each of the colours to be printed.

Series A number of founts of different sizes of the same typeface.

Serif A small terminal stroke at the end of the main stroke of a letter.

Set The width of each individual character in a typeface. The average set is used for copyfitting.

Sewing Binding involving the sewing of sections together with thread, before a paperback or hard cover is glued on.

Sheet fed Printing press where paper is fed in as single sheets, rather than on a roll.

Silk screen A printing process where ink is forced through a stencil placed on a fine mesh screen.

Spiral/wire comb/plastic comb binding Binding process where holes are punched in a set of collated sheets and a wire or plastic coil or comb is inserted.

Spread Any left and right pair of facing pages.

S/S Abbreviation for same size.

Stab stitching Binding where staples are punched into the side of a publication, close to the spine, usually then covered with a glued-on cover.

Stet An instruction to ignore a previously marked correction.

Subheading Heading in text marking a new section inside a chapter.

Tail The margin between the printed image and the foot of a page.

Tint A ready-made dotted pattern, in various densities, used to give a lighter version of the colour being used for printing. Sometimes called a mechanical tint.

Title page The page containing the title of a book, author's and publisher's names, etc., appearing at the front of a book or pamphlet. Can be preceded by a *half-title*.

Title-page verso The reverse of a title page, usually used for copyright and bibliographical information.

Top The margin between the printed image and the top of a page.

Typescript The raw written material for a publication, as submitted by the author.

U/lc Abbreviation instructing the typesetter to use initial capitals for proper names, etc., with lower case for the rest of the word.

Varnishing Process of printing a clear varnish over a cover, etc. for protection.

Verso Left-hand page.

Web fed Printing press where paper is fed in on a roll or web.

White line Line in the text consisting only of space.

Widow Short line at the foot of a page or column which will look better if it is moved. An orphan is the same thing at the top of a page.

Work and turn Imposition whereby a sheet of paper is printed on both sides from the same plate.

x-height The height of the lower case x, and other characters without ascenders or descenders, in a typeface.

Xerography Printing process where powder is deposited on a surface under electrostatic charge and fused by a heater. The image is created by light through a combination of lenses and mirrors.

Index